MOUNTAIN BIKE GUIDE

THE NORTH MIDLANDS: MANCHESTER, CHESHIRE & STAFFORDSHIRE

By Henry Tindell

The Ernest Press
www.ernest-press.co.uk

Published by the Ernest Press 2005
© Copyright Henry Tindell

ISBN: 0 948153 77 6

Typeset by Phil Hodgkiss Design & Print

CHAPTER	CONTENTS	PAGE

NORTH MIDLANDS MOUNTAIN BIKING - ROUTE STATISTICS

NO.	ROUTE	winter	rating	grade	dist. miles	ht.gain feet	off-rd. %age	time
GTR. MANCHESTER								
1	Werneth Low	W	*	Mod	17	950	55	2.5
2	Mellor Moor		***	Diff	17	1700	69	3.5
3	Winter Hill		*	Mod+	20	875	30	3.25
4	Anglezarke	W	**	Mod+	13	950	65	2.25
5	Windy Hill		***	Diff-	18	1650	40	3.5
CHESHIRE								
6	Lyme Park	W	*	Mod	16.5	1050	61	2.75
7	Kerridge Hill		**	Diff+	22.5	1150	32	3.5
8	Alderley Edge	W	*	Mod	13.5	450	24	2.75
9	Dunham Massey	W	*	Mod	20	150	55	2.5
10	Tatton Park		*	Mod	21	300	41	3.25
11	Helsby Hill		*	Mod+	16	500	38	2.5
12	Mow Cop	W	*	Mod	14.5	950	44	3
STAFFORDSHIRE								
13	Rushton Spencer		**	Mod+	16	1100	47	2.5
14	Morridge Hill		*	Mod+	18.75	2350	21	3
15	Derbyshire Bridge		***	Diff	21	2750	42	4.5
16	Keele		*	Mod+	20	750	47	3
17	Hanbury Hill		*	Mod	13	450	23	2.25
18	Churnet Valley		**	Mod+	16	750	58	3
19	Abbott's Bromley		*	Mod	18	600	30	3
20	Downs Banks	W	**	Mod+	13	750	40	2.25
21	Stafford Castle		*	Diff-	23	525	52	3.75
22	Shugborough		*	Mod+	15	650	62	2.5
CHES. - STAFFS.								
23 o	Macclesfield - Alton (YHA)	W	***	Diff-	33	2475	40	5
23 r	Alton (YHA) - Macclesfield		**	Diff+	39	3225	25	8
24	Macc. - Alton - Macc.		***	Sev-	72	5700	33	13

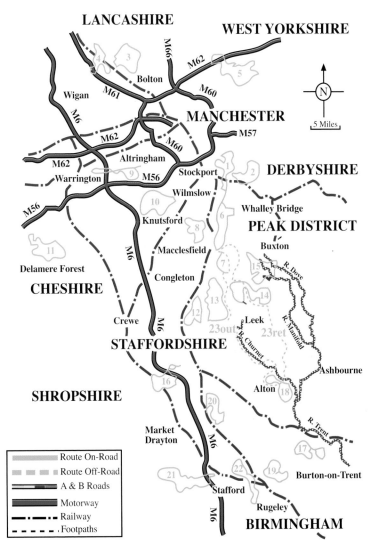

LANCASHIRE

WEST YORKSHIRE

M66

M62

Bolton

M61

M60

Wigan

MANCHESTER

M6

M57

M62

M60

Altringham

M62

Warrington

M56

M56

Stockport

DERBYSHIRE

Wilmslow

Knutsford

Whalley Bridge

PEAK DISTRICT

Delamere Forest

Buxton

CHESHIRE

Macclesfield

R. Dove

Congleton

R. Manifold

Crewe

Leek

R. Churnet

23out

23ret

STAFFORDSHIRE

Ashbourne

SHROPSHIRE

Alton

R. Trent

Market
Drayton

M6

Burton-on-Trent

Stafford

BIRMINGHAM

Rugeley

M6

N

5 Miles

Route On-Road
Route Off-Road
A & B Roads
Motorway
Railway
Footpaths

ABBREVIATIONS

TL	Turn Left
TR	Turn Right
SO	Straight On
T-jn	T-junction
X-rd	Cross-road
ln	lane
rd	road
Fm	farm
SP	sign post
FP	footpath
BW	bridleway
(W)	route passable in winter conditions
mls	miles – normal unit of distance (eg. 2mls)
m	metres – normal short distance (eg. 100m)
ft	feet – normal measure of height (eg. 975ft)

MAPS

Note, check orientation as north is not always to top of the page. Approximate scales, orientation, features, topography and layout are for guidance. All routes should be reviewed against the relevant OS map. (1:50 000 Landranger, or 1:25 000 Leisure/Explorer series – see route info). The following LR maps cover the region:-

- **109**	**Manchester**	- **117**	**Chester**
- **118**	**Stoke-on-Trent**	- **119**	**Buxton**
- **127**	**Stafford**	- **128**	**Derby**

BIBLIOGRAPHY

- Walking in Staffordshire, Julie Meech, Cicerone Press
- The Treasures of Cheshire, North West Civic Trust
- The Treasures of Lancashire, North West Civic Trust
- The Village Atlas (growth of S Lancs / N Ches, 1840 – 1920), Alderman Press
- Staffordshire (Rock climbs), British Mountaineering Council

PROLOGUE

Bang! As I sailed past the gaggle of golfers about to tee off – making my way swiftly downhill after the delightful bridleway high over the M62 – I was as surprised as they were by the loud retort as my rear tyre exploded.

Grateful for a soft landing, I managed to disembark with some decorum, declining Pete and Martin's offer to ride back for a lift. After some rather Heath-Robinson repairs, my spare tube barely grinned through the rent in the tyre wall – the meagre inflation just enabling a canny finish to the ride, along the last couple of miles back to Hollingworth Lake (on route no.5).

This nicely epitomised for me the ephemeral fun of Mountain Biking in the North Midlands – having just puffed up to the magnificent moorland views from Windy Hill, swooped back down to the valley, and trundled up and down the glorious gritstone pavé of its remote drystone-walled bridleways. Escaping the soon-to-break weather, enjoying the companionship, and even the tyre failure added a piquancy to the outing – that can make the mundane memorable, even for an ordinary route (which this particular one certainly was not!).

The point is that the élan of Mountain Biking in the North Midlands can be discovered not just from some rather fine tracks and vistas (as in the multi-starred routes), but just as well for the more modest (single star) rides. Given the right circumstances such as riding companions, weather, need to get-away-from-it-all, or whatever ... the right approach is everything.

I hope that you enjoy these rides as much as I do!

Henry Tindell,
Cheadle Hulme, 2004.

ACKNOWLEDGEMENTS

Firstly, Ernest Press Editor, Peter Hodgkiss for his steadfast support of what has turned out to be a rather long-running project; and latterly Phil Hodgkiss for his efforts – pity the weather beat us on route 24! My family, Susan, Richard and Alistair, without whom I would never have started it in the first place – or finally finished it. Bill and Mo for after-work therapy on Winter Hill. True cycling (and tearoom) enthusiasts from the Cheshire section of the Veteran Cycling Club for (unwittingly!) testing parts of the Cheshire routes. And especially Pete, Martin and Martin for (wittingly!) exploring some of the tougher routes and sharing some great days out – to all, I hope there are many more to come!

PREFACE

Around the North Midlands.

Beyond the high regions of England and Wales, Mountain Biking in the North Midlands encompasses many of the best aspects of its genre. Un-rivalled access from Manchester and Birmingham makes a number of summer evening rides viable from these centres. The terrain is certainly varied – ranging from the fringe of the West Pennine Moors (north of Manchester); the gritstone moors south-east of Manchester; wooded hills and tracks from the leafy suburbs of south Manchester; rugged hills at the edge of the Peak from Macclesfield; the sandstone outcrops of the mid-Cheshire ridge from Helsby Hill southwards; lowland bridleways of rural Cheshire and Staffordshire; 'little Bavaria' of the Churnet Val-ley; to the edge of Cannock Chase, marking the beginning of the West Midlands.

A view from the hills.

Although the peaks are not particularly high, the routes lead to some superb vantage points, important since prehistoric times. At the Iron Age fort of Helsby Hill (route 11) we can pick out Winter Hill (route 3, and Rivington Pike, route 4), 25 miles north-west. On Winter Hill the view south reveals Lyme Park (route 6), 25 miles away. Five miles from Lyme is seen the prominent ridge of Kerridge Hill (route 7), above Bollington. The curious White Nancy, atop Kerridge Hill looks to Sutton Tower, on route 7, some five miles away, beyond Macclesfield.

Sutton Tower has a view west to the Cat and Fiddle (route 15), which in turn overlooks the Peak District including southeastwards six miles to Morridge Hill and the Mermaid Inn (route 14). From the Mermaid the view west, over the Roaches, leads to the hilltop folly of Mow Cop and Bosley Cloud, (route 14). Ten miles north from Mow lies Alderley Edge, of route 8 – with Helsby Hill in its vista, some 20 miles northwest – thus completing a magnificent hilltop circumnavigation around the heart of the North Midlands.

Grand views encourage a special empathy with the landscape well-known to travellers in ages past, important not only to literally see 'the lie of the land', but as a communication chain. Beacon to beacon, they carried the news of great events where now radio and satellite masts stand. A reminder of the four-thousand-year span since the intensive husbandry of the land in the Bronze Age – only in the past couple of hundred years have we enjoyed the luxury of accurate maps ... Looking across these landscapes from our hilltops thus reminds us of the wonderful three-dimensional perspective still to be discovered at first-hand; beyond the two-dimensional map and photograph are hills particularly appropriate to mountain biking.

INTRODUCTION
North Midlands Mountain Biking

The great conurbations of the North Midlands, from Manchester in the north to Birmingham in the south, provide particularly easy access to these routes. The general tranquillity of the rides contradict the fact that the M6 or M62 are seldom more than a dozen miles away, and many routes can be comfortably started from the railway network. Whilst it is likely that the majority will need only to travel relatively short distances to their chosen routes, the region deserves a visit from further afield as it is generously endowed with places of interest, welcoming hostelries, and accommodation to suit all tastes – near to the 'honeypot' centres of the Peak District, Alton Towers and Cannock Chase. The final route could make an overnight stop at mid-distance in the Churnet Valley (at Alton YHA), making an engaging weekend expedition – or very long and challenging day-return.

Mountain Biking in the North Midlands complements the series of established Ernest Press Mountain Bike Guides, with the routes described to the north-east of Manchester approaching the West Yorkshire book. Around south-east Manchester/north-east Cheshire, the routes adjoin the two Derbyshire/Peak District guides. In the west, beyond the Cheshire plain, the Mid-Wales guide takes over. Staffordshire provides routes as far south as Cannock, where the West Midlands guide begins.

A surprising range of difficulty and terrain is to be found within Greater Manchester, Cheshire and Staffordshire. As these may not be areas immediately associated with appealing off-road riding, a principal aim is to demonstrate its (largely untapped) potential. From bases such as Bolton or Macclesfield, fine routes are available to take the pressure off the honeypot regions of the Peak.

Manchester is a remarkably convenient base from which to reach some exceptional countryside – from Rivington (route 4), twelve miles to its north-west; Winter Hill (route 3) ten miles north; to the Saddleworth moors (route 5) ten miles east. Ten miles south-east of the centre leads to the suburban fringe of Romily and Marple, inclining towards the genuine gritstone moorlands on Werneth Low and Mellor Moor (routes 1 and 2).

Cheshire is a county of many faces, from the well-known 'northern home-counties' of its flourishing medieval towns and pastoral farmlands to the huge chemical complexes of the Dee estuary in the north-west and the hill-country of the east. The mid-Cheshire ridge (of sandstone) provides iron-age hill-fort locations for rides at Helsby Hill (route 11) in the north, to Mow Cop (route 12) in the south. The 'stockbroker belt' of Wilmslow and Alderley Edge (routes 8 and 10), perhaps surprisingly, produces an excellent introduction to off-road riding with more moderate gradients, and tracks linked by delightful leafy country lanes.

East Cheshire contains the real hills that rise from Bollington and Macclesfield; this is true gritstone country at the edge of the Peak District. The highest village (Flash) and second-highest inn (The Cat and Fiddle) in England – the latter still in Cheshire – are passed on the Derbyshire Bridge route (15) that visits the junction of Cheshire, Derbyshire and Staffordshire at Three Shires Head for a brief and un-missable foray around these borders. A high gritstone and moorland route that encompasses the source of five of the Peak's great rivers – Dove, Manifold, Wye, Dane and Goyt.

Staffordshire rides include the renowned Staffordshire Moorlands, surprisingly on routes generally outside the Peak, visiting The Mermaid at Morridge Moor (route 14) – the third highest pub in England. That just leaves The Tan Inn as the highest, (but it **is** one hundred miles up the Pennines in the wilds of the North Riding of Yorkshire). The source of the River Churnet is passed en-route, near Royal Cottage. It flows around Leek and The Roaches to Tittersworth Reservoir, before heading down the heavily wooded Churnet Valley to Alton and eventually feeding the Trent.

There are delightful surprises in 'Rhineland' as the Churnet Valley winds below Alton Towers on route 18. Some fine rolling countryside and tracks are found around the Potteries at Stoke-on-Trent, Stafford and Stone, (routes 16, 20 and 21). Travelling east towards Burton-on-Trent, the Trent valley provides open country and varied bridleways near Blithefield Reservoir (route 19). Nearby is Abbots Bromley, famous for its medieval Horn Dance, performed in September; whilst Hanbury (route 17) lies on an escarpment with surrounding villages in a clay-land where riding and rain are best kept well apart!

Ten miles north of Birmingham lies Cannock Chase where route 22 crosses the old Essex Bridge to Shugborough Park, leading to the Chase and a profusion of bridleways that provide for family outings as well as tougher rides. **Ches – Staffs.** Complementing the circular routes, a marathon weekend ride from Macclesfield tackles the stiff east Cheshire hills, then drops down to Rudyard Lake, to follow the Churnet Valley to an overnight stop at The Ranger (YHA), Dimmingsdale, near Alton, as route 23 (out). The return passes Alton Towers and rises to a long ride across the Staffordshire Moorlands, outside the Peak, to The Mermaid Inn on Morridge Moor. Descending the Moor, around the Roaches and into the Dane Valley, the lanes follow the valley before the final high point at Macclesfield Forest – superb views. Route 24 combines the last two, possible in one push for those seeking a suitably challenging finalé.

GRADING

The rides are graded for length, height gain, difficulty and 'quality', which despite subjectivity should enable a reasonable estimate of the commitment required before tackling them. Although naturally benefiting from good weather, those marked 'W' (winter) are normally passable even under adverse conditions (some I've even traversed in 'Arctic' conditions). The remainder generally contain only short stretches problematic in the wet – such as traversing ploughed fields or boggy ground, where a carry is advisable, although appropriate diversions are noted. Only on the Kerridge Hill and Hanbury Hills routes are there serious stretches of severely muddy going, only to be tackled in dry conditions (or hard frozen, for the experienced!).

Times stated should be treated with caution until adjusted to individual style – often route-finding can be the critical element, and a fair safety factor should always be built in, to cope with local difficulties like punctures, synonymous with hawthorn hedges!

It is **strongly recommended** that the chosen routes be reviewed on an OS 1:50 000 (Landranger series) or 1:25 000 (Leisure series) map. These provide invaluable information about the area and form an essential part of any sensible country-goer's equipment – vital preparation.

GEARING UP

Equipment and clothing can reflect the difficulty and length of the routes, and although full mountain bike spec. and equipment is appropriate for the more serious routes, the easier ones can be undertaken (with obvious care and eye on the weather) as family outings, with the minimum of gear. Although the routes are neither as remote nor arduous as the mountain areas of Britain, being caught by bad weather or vanishing light can still be unpleasant, at the least. For the more adventurous the fine line between risk and reward can only be gained by hard experience; but the satisfaction in finally finding a way though difficult ground just before resources or the light fails (or the pub closes!) is known to all true hill-travellers of bridleway, footpath or crag.

As a guide, for dry-ish summer conditions I use a light, long-zipped cycling top, or similar; shorts or cycling longs; trainers – normally dispensing with gloves, never without glasses. Absolutely no-one would fail to advocate using a modern helmet, being light, stylish and generally *de-rigueur*. A substantial bum-bag may be sufficient, but I almost never venture out without my faithful old rucksack – containing map(s) and basic tool kit, comprising spare tube, link extractor, puncture outfit, two small adjustable spanners, two screwdrivers (double as tyre levers), Allen keys, copper wire, string, rubber bands (cut from old inner tubes), and gaffer tape plus pump, and finally cable and lock for securing the machine. A light cag, spare pullover and small towel, with a basic first-aid kit are all kept in the 'sack. I also have at least one camera and spare film, and some 'emergency rations', including cash, all habitually taken on almost every substantial ride.

In more adverse conditions, clothing is varied accordingly, my preference being for heavy-duty calf-length gaiters and walking boots below; Lifa base layer, covered by a Polartec-type fleece and a light breathable cag on top – normally sufficient down towards zero. Even subzero is quite feasible with only minor additions (another base layer, better gloves and headgear) as proven on routes 7 and 8, enjoyed in severe midwinter conditions – providing one can keep moving comfortably!

MACHINE PREPARATION

Keep all moving parts liberally lubricated, especially the hard-working drivetrain and cables. Saddle height should allow (while sitting on the saddle) comfortable reach of the pedal in it's downward stroke with the ball of the foot and without preventing the ground being reached 'in-extremis'.

Similarly, tyre pressure should be high enough to reduce rolling resistance on the Tarmac whilst permitting some shock absorption off-road. All non-vital equipment ('unsprung weight') should be shed from the bike, and a Karrimat-type padding around the frame greatly reduces the pain for enforced carries. I much prefer to lift over all muddy ground, as once the chain is contaminated further progress is made only at the cost of dramatically reduced efficiency.

Choice of machine is naturally subjective, but these routes can mostly be tackled with a fairly wide range – my preference being for simplicity and lightness, with comfortably large tyre sections – reliability and durability being the most valuable characteristics. Whilst the more arduous demand a decent mountain bike, the easier routes can (and have!) been happily traversed, albeit usually under favourable conditions, on machines ranging from my hack touring bike to an Edwardian Triumph roadster, courtesy of the Veteran Cycle Club.

RIGHTS OF WAY

ROWs are crucial to continuing access, and everything possible must be done by all participants to avoid jeopardizing them, or antagonizing others met in the country. The first principle is to be fully aware of ROW status, and defer to other users – giving way to people on foot or horseback. Take particular care when approaching from behind – always give plenty of gentle warning, go slowly or pull up. Common sense and courtesy must prevail at all times, even if one cannot concur with views of others such as farmers or landowners. Always give way and if necessary retreat and avoid confrontation – always a good option by bike!

The basics of ROWs are:-

Footpaths: These are the province of those on foot only. Pushing or carrying a bike is normally acceptable, but riding is **definitely not**, and is a 'civil wrong' which could result in being sued as a civil offence. Observing the approach above should enable one to travel safely throughout the countryside encountered in this book.

Bridleways: Since 1968 these have been open to cyclists, and horse riders, **but** the former must always give way to the latter, **and** to those on foot. Motorised vehicles are **not** legally permitted.

Permissive paths: Specially-designated by the landowner, these have the same status as normal, (in this case bridleway). However, they can be withdrawn, so the above comments are particularly important. A good example is the enlightened approach to permissive paths (bridleway and footpath) which has opened up Winter Hill, Bolton, where in previous generations it was restricted to grouse-shooting parties – there is a clear responsibility for all country-goers to assist this trend.

RUPP / BOAT: Roads Used as Public Paths / Byways Open to All Traffic are relatively rare in this region, but access by cyclists presents no problems. Other traffic may legally use, but has often led to severe damage to tracks attacked irresponsibly by 4-WDs – a lesson for the way we must treat bridleways, as there is no excuse for spoiling any track by passage of rider and bike.

Unclassified Roads: Often known as 'White Roads' are normally accessible to cyclists, but to be sure the local authority Definitive Map must be consulted.

Canal Towpaths: These are a tremendous resource for the cyclist, but there are some simple precautions – generally owned by British Waterways, a visit to the web-site provides a free permit by simply registering. All that is required is to display the permit, and check that the path chosen is approved – in practice this should be OK as British Waterways make every effort to open them to cyclists wherever practical but one can easily make sure (www.countryside.gov.uk).

THE COUNTRY CODE

The above should be sufficient to ensure that no aspect of the countryside is upset whilst we enjoy its facilities, but the established Country Code is worthy of reproduction from www.countryside.gov.uk:-

* Be safe – plan ahead and follow any signs
* Leave gates and property as you find them
* Protect plants and animals, and take your litter home
* Keep dogs under close control
* Consider other people

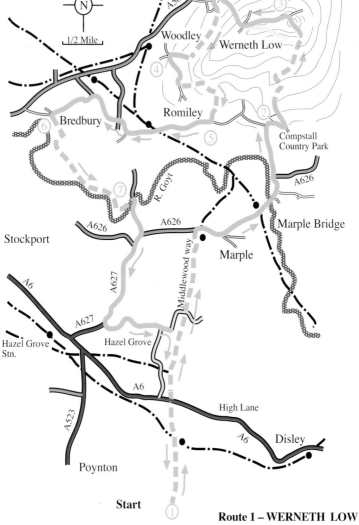

Start

Route 1 – WERNETH LOW

Route 1	**Werneth Low**

Distance:	17mls.
Off-road:	55%
Height gain:	950 feet
Time:	2^1/$_2$hrs.
Grade:	Moderate (+)
Rating:	* (W)
Refreshments:	Café and pub at start, Marple Bridge & Romily, pub at Marple & Compstall.
Railway:	Poynton station, (2mls.). Passes Marple and Romily Stns.
Start:	Nelson Pit Visitor Centre, Anson Rd., Higher Poynton, Ches. GR: 934 844
Map:	LR 109 (Manchester); Dark Peak /Explorer 277 1:25 000.

Summary:

A good introductory route, rideable throughout the year. Good tracks, but care required on the return road if busy. Climb to Werneth Low provides the only significant gradient, not too demanding. A worthwhile outing, with excellent refreshment opportunities!

Route:

1 – 2

Down to the Middlewood Way, opposite the Boars Head, and under the bridge; continuing along the disused railway track to its terminus at Rose Hill station, Marple. Exit rather inauspiciously by the waste tip, following the lane to T-jn with main road. TR, follow towards Marple then TL at first lights. After a rise, steeply down into Marple Bridge, past canal and station to the lights at the bottom – TL (opposite the Norfolk Arms) and along Lower Fold. SO at next jn., following B6104 (towards Romily). Downhill to Compstall, TR at SP 'Etherow Country Park', along George St.

2 – 3

Past the Country Park (café) and TL at the fork, rising past The Andrew Arms, then TL after the Methodist Church, into John St. Uphill, now School Lane, as track becomes semi-metalled past School Lane Fm. TR after Hydes Fm. into Beacon Ln (BW SP). Follow track to the top, and fine views.

3 – 4

SO, alongside golf course and communication masts, and downhill past golf clubhouse, to T-jn. TR, down Joel Lane. At bottom, T-jn, TL, and immediately TL again, into Wych Fold. TL into Hudson Rd. Continue (now Derby Rd.), and SO, following SP 'Woodley $3/4$' (SP states 'FP' – actually BW). SO, (SP 'Woodley') – fine track until reach metalled lane, leading to T-jn.

4 – 5

TL, (exiting Hillside Rd.), along Werneth Rd. Into Greave and TL (after Foresters Arms) into Pinfold Lane, becoming BW track thro' wood. SO (main track), down to small metalled lane to T-jn.

5 – 6

TL, (exiting Heys Ln.), downhill to meet main road to Romily. TR (opposite is the Cherry Tree). Past Romily Stn., SO at lights, along Berrycroft Ln., then Bents Ln. TL (at Queens pub) along Vernon Rd. TR into Park Rd, now into Bredbury. TL, down Kingsway (not signed), and past The Yew Tree. Down and TL at SP 'Bredbury Hall Country Club'.

6 – 7

This is Dark Ln. (unmarked), SO (SP 'BW 56'), good track, and past Goyt Hall Fm; nearby is River Goyt. Emerge at T-jn with road, (SP 'BW 56').

7 – 8

TR, following road past the Hare and Hounds to lights at T-jn. TR, towards Stockport, on A626. Up to lights (100m) and TL, along A627, towards Hazel Grove. Past Stockport Golf Club and 'S' bends to TL into Torkington Rd. Heading into country, at the sharp L bend of Oak Cottage, continue by **pushing** the 20m along the FP leading to the Middlewood Way.

8 – 1

TR, following the trail directly back to the start, having passed under the A6 at High Lane. Refreshments at Boars Head or café, visitors centre, picnic tables and canal basin, make this a popular rendezvous.

Ascending Werneth Low, from Compstall - enthusiasm more important than machinery or age (route 1)

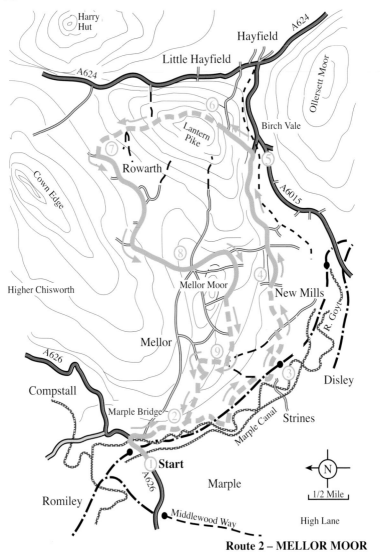

Route 2 – MELLOR MOOR

Route 2	**Mellor Moor**
Distance:	17mls.
Off-road:	69%
Height gain:	1,700 feet
Time:	3$^1/_2$hrs.
Grade:	Difficult
Rating:	***
Refreshments:	Café and pub at Marple Bridge, café at Roman Lakes, restaurant at Rowarth, several pubs around route (see text).
Railway :	Marple Bridge station, (start).
Map:	LR 109 (Manchester); Dark Peak, 1:25 000
Start:	Marple Bridge (free) carpark, near canal. GR:963893

Summary:

A fine ride, from the country town of Marple Bridge into the Goyt and Sett valleys along good lowland bridleways, leading to the edge of the western Peak's gritstone moorland. Distant views towards Kinder Scout are left for a return via the isolated hamlet of Rowarth, and finish on interesting tracks. Demands a degree of experience to cope with deceptively hilly and rugged country with some magnificent tracks providing appropriate reward.

Route:

1 – 2

TR out of the carpark, heading steeply downhill to the lights at the bottom. TR along the fine little street, replete with pubs and café. 100m after the lights TR into Low Lea Rd. The lane rises stiffly and becomes semi-metalled as it eases down towards the Roman Lakes, via a TL and then TR before the Fm, following Lakes Rd.

2 – 3

Past the Lake, at the end of which is the café. SO, (BW SP), following the River Goyt, and under the impressive viaduct. SO along the excellent track, thro' tunnel to the second gate, leading onto a metalled lane, several SP's (BW, etc.). TR, following lane, over railway track and past Fm, to T-jn. TL, uphill over cobbles to Strines station, still on 'Goyt Way'.

3 – 4

Fork L, thro' tunnel and past station on R, then fork R, uphill steadily on a superb track – a test of skill and stamina! Finally exit at jn with road at 'phone box and enticing Fox Inn. TR up lane, then TL into first track (crossing), a magnificent example of gritstone that is just-rideable all the way. Passing the golf course, the surface becomes easier as the top is reached at the clubhouse and crossing of a lane. Distant views of Kinder, ahead.

4 – 5

SO, and downhill along Apple Tree Rd., towards New Mills. SO, down Watford Rd., to T-jn at bottom and TL along Batemill Rd. Continue past The Printer's Arms and then Sycamore Rd. past The Sycamore Inn, to finally downhill and TL into the BW at 'Spinny Cottage', (BW SP, but easily missed) leading steadily uphill.

5 – 6

The drystone-walled and cobbled BW soon defers to a less uniform surface and a push. SO thro' gate, then keep to the L (higher) track, now providing excellent views over the Sett valley and Peak. Past Higginbottom Fm, SO over lane crossing, following BW SP and past 'Windy Knoll'. SO at fork, as BW SP, now on unmade track - real MTB ground! SO thro' gate at NT 'Lantern Pike' plaque.

6 – 7

Follow BW SP, alongside drystone wall, varying surface requiring some cunning. SO over top to finally exit thro' gate at 'Lantern Pike' SP. Into the open field (no track), trending a little L to pick up the track leading to Blackstone Fm, down to the field corner, several SPs. TL into Monks Rd, a drystone walled, stony track. SO, thro' two gates, downhill to T-jn with metalled lane, and TL.

7 – 8

SO, down to Back Rowarth, BW SPs, fording stream, good track. Over rise onto semi-metalled track and TL, downhill to reach metalled lane to Rowarth. To L is Little Mill restaurant and Rowarth hamlet, but continue SO to the T-jn, TR (SP 'New Mills') then past the 'Childrens Inn' (now private house). Steadily up to T-jn, TL (SP 'New Mills'). Past the Moorfield Arms, (with further fine views over Kinder, on L). At the six-way (road & track) jn, exit Shiloh Rd by taking the most central, SO along the loose-stone surfaced, walled track.

8 – 9

Past the high bank of reservoir (SP 'Derbyshire Wildlife Trust'). Just before the cottage, TR at track crossing, gently rising to the high point. TL into track joining from L, going due west (into evening sun), following SP 'Strines'. 100m of rather muddy going can be avoided with cunning, past the (easily missed) trig point. Begin to descend, to steep, stony track, SO over metalled lane crossing. Continue SO down the steadily narrowing track, culminating in a boulder-filled high-banked and enclosed track that was just beyond my riding abilities – but only a short dismount, to the crossing of a metalled lane – super! TR and thro' the golf course on the lane.

9 – 1

Past the ostrich farm(!), traversing the hillside to the T-jn, TL. 'Mellor & Townscliffe' golf clubhouse passed, then TL down the metalled track, passing the Scout Camp (Linnet Clough). SO as the track becomes unsurfaced, delightfully interesting yet rideable with care, down to exit at the Fm by the Roman Lakes, where the outward route is retraced. At T-jn TR, along Bottom Mill Rd., up the rise then down to a TL into Marple Bridge. Along Town St. for 100m where TL and 50m steeply uphill returns to the start.

A little gem, perfect for a balmy summer evening.

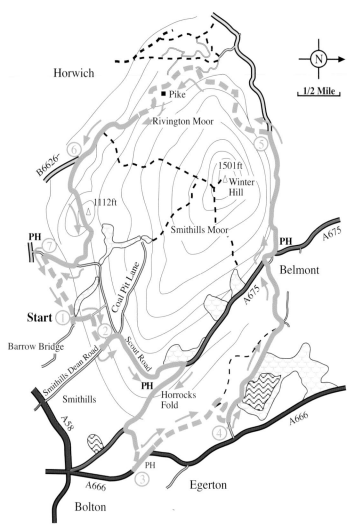

Route 3 – WINTER HILL

Route 3   **Winter Hill**

Distance:	20mls.
Off-road:	30%
Height gain:	875 feet
Time:	3$^{1}/_{4}$hrs.
Grade:	Moderate
Rating:	* (W)
Refreshments:	Cafe off-route at Rivington; refreshments at Bryan Hey Fm, Scout Rd.; Black Dog at Belmont; Wilton Arms on A675; providing, at various times, for the hungry hill-goer.
Railway:	Bolton station, central Bolton, 3mls. from start – OK by bike.
Start:	Barrow Bridge carpark, Smithills, (NW Bolton). GR: 687117
Map:	LR 109 (Manchester); Explorer 19 (West Pennine Moors), 1:25 000.

Summary:

A route passable throughout the year, providing a circumnavigation of Winter Hill (1500ft) and good views south over Bolton, Manchester and a distant Peak District. The great mast of Winter Hill is easily visible from upland Cheshire 30 miles distant. Tracks generally excellent, but the linking roads require care, thereby loosing stars.

Route:

1 – 2

TL out of the secluded (free) carpark, following the tiny lane past the fine old mill managers' cottages and around the sharp bend (the return route rejoins here), then uphill until TR into the BW (SP 'Smithills Dean Rd.'). Good track, past Pendlebury's Fm, fenced BW continues gently down to exit at T-jn with Smithills Dean Rd. TL, going uphill.

2 – 3

Up to T-jn, TR along Scout Rd, traversing around the hill, then down past Wilton Quarries (long-standing forcing ground for Bolton rock climbers), to T-jn with the A675 – great care here! Thankfully gradient-assisted, past Wilton Arms, to TL into Templecombe Dr. TR at 2nd Midford Dr. TL into Masbury Close, then immediately TR along semi-metalled track, and easily down in 200m to T-jn with Bolton – Blackburn Rd, (exiting Springfield Rd.) at Dunscar.

3 – 4

TL, at The Cheetham Arms, downhill on the main road thankfully soon quitted by continuing SO along the track, behind the large house, as the road bends R. A good, semi-metalled track, but no SPs (although a BW). SO (ignoring a L), then fork R, on lower track. SO, past golf course (ignoring L fork), occasional BW SP, to gate at stream crossing. TR (acute), now **pushing** the 200m up the broad track as FP status, to reach road 100m beyond next gate. Careful bike lift required over this gate, then walk thro' swing gate beside – the only awkward part of the route.

4 – 5

At road TL, and past 'Blackburn with Darwin' SP – on L lies eastern profile of Winter Hill. Past Delph Sailing club, to X-Rd where TL to Belmont. Swiftly down, taking L fork and exiting Egerton Rd. at T-jn with A675. TR, then shortly TL at The Black Dog (sometime base for the Belmont Winter Hill Fell Race each May). Steeply up Church St., leaving Belmont as gradient eases but climb continues, the moorland lane traversing the north of Winter Hill. Just beyond the crest, past SP 'Chorley, Rivington', TL into the obvious track, SP 'concessionary BW' – brilliant moorland track.

5 – 6

SO along track, affording magnificent views west over plains of Lancashire, as Rivington Pike is visited by following the BW L around the tower, then rapidly down to rejoin the main track. The Isle of Man reputably visible from the Pike, but immediate interest lies with a glorious descent of the track, past Pike Cottage, finally emerging onto the metalled lane, clear views over Reebock stadium at Horwich as head around to south flank of Winter Hill. Past the houses, along the parallel lane and TL into Matchmoor Lane.

6 – 7

Along the gentle but insidious rise of Matchmoor Lane, finally over the rise (Trig. Point nearby), then down to T-jn. TR (care!), uphill then down, almost to Bob's Smithy (pub, with food, at X-rds,), to TL into the BW, (obvious BW track, with barrier but no SP) leading across the golf course.

7 – 1

SO, excellent cobbled track, past clubhouse, then TL at fork, leading to fine narrow track, quickly down to reach the road at Barrow Bridge. SO, back to start to complete the circuit of Bolton's finest asset – viva Winter Hill!

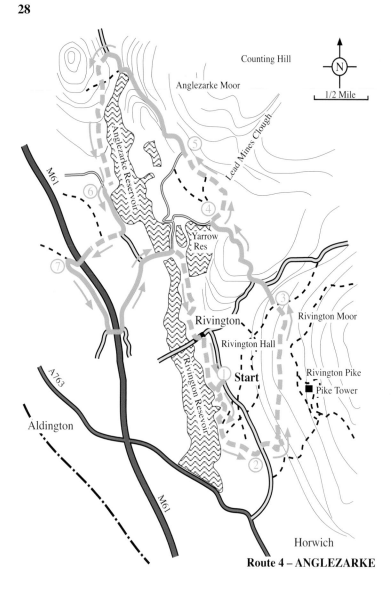

Route 4 – ANGLEZARKE

Route 4   **Anglezarke**

Distance:	13mls.
Off-road:	65%
Height gain:	950 feet
Time:	2¼hrs.
Grade:	Moderate (+)
Rating:	** (W)
Refreshments:	Rivington Great Barn (café), pubs around route (see text).
Railway :	Adlington or Horwich (Bolton to Blackpool N-line) one to two miles from route.
Start:	Rivington Great Barn (parking), Rivington: 6 mls. NW of Bolton. GR629138
Map:	LR 109 (Manchester); Explorer 19 (West Pennine Moors), 1:25 000.

Summary:
A splendid little route, a justifiably popular area, only a mile or two from Horwich and jn 6 of the M61, yet this is true Lancashire gritstone country. Skirts the great uplands of Anglezarke Moor in the West Pennine Moors. The fine village of Rivington and the extensive reservoirs combine with facilities at the Great Barn and mansion, Rivington Pike and unique country parkland bequeathed by a local lad made good. Harold Lever (Lord Leverhulme), who began his still-flourishing industrial empire from a stall in his birthplace of Bolton, finally owned all of the land from Rivington Reservoir to the Pike – providing the well-regarded course for the 2002 Commonwealth Games Mountain Biking events. Excellent tracks throughout, a great place for an evening ride, thereby avoiding the busiest times during summer.

Route:

1 – 2

From the Great Barn, head towards the lake, thro' the trees, following BW SP. TL following fence around the lakeside on a good track that leads pleasantly in and out the wood until the 'ruined castle' is reached – a rich man's folly, replica of the long-gone Liverpool castle. TL here, following the tree-lined boulevard (BW!) to the crossing of the road.

2 – 3

Just before the road, TL opposite the carpark, cutting off the corner, to exit by crossing the road and following the BW SP directly into the holly copse and alongside the school houses. Up the sunken track (possibly muddy in wet conditions), thro' gate and superb leafmold surface to meet a broad gravel track (T-jn). TL, and then in 50m TR (acute) past three posts (possible soft ground) on broad track (no SP) shortly to meet next track (T-jn). TL, and then thro' gate (SP 'concessionary BW'). Mountain biking track *par excellence,* rough stony surface, steadily inclining yet rideable all the way with determination ... SO, over BW crossings, on main track, through masses of rhododendrons. Finally over the rise, down large gritstone setts and under the curious stone bridge (this was the Chinese Garden and Pigeon Tower area). Steadily down, until suddenly expansive views over the lakes are revealed as the carpark is reached. Ahead lies Anglezarke Moor.

3 – 4

SO thro' the carpark and down the metalled lane. SO to 2nd jn and TR, going smartly downhill (14% SP) and past Wilcocks Fm, built 1670. SO down next (17%) hill, and to the small bridge over the reservoir neck.

4 – 5

Immediately over the bridge, TR into the obvious track (BW SP). Delightful wall/tree-lined track to Lead Mines Clough. Over a bridge, alongside stream, then after 150m TL, following track across the stream as it zig-zags steeply up to gate (BW SP). SO, keeping hard by the fence on R of field, exemplary BW SPs! SO, now on track over the rise, and gates, to emerge at apex of metalled lane.

5 – 6

TR, heading downhill past Manor House on a fast descent (17%), crossing yet another reservoir end, as begin the rise of Higher House Ln. At the Fm (date-stone inscription 'TARM 1696') TL into the small BW (SP). Great little track leading uphill, proves just too tricky to ride throughout. As it flattens out, the riding is enjoyable, with views over the water to Anglezarke, Winter Hill and Rivington Pike. SO, past concessionary BW that provides an optional extra of visiting Chorley Nab (pleasant little diversion - allow 20mins). Fine, sandy track gently down to Kay's Fm, where TR onto small concrete lane for 100m to T-jn with metalled lane.

6 – 7

TL, and along to bends and Taylors Fm, where TR (BW SP). Nice little track following stream down to the small footbridge, followed across the stream. Sunken track rises up pleasantly, soon arriving at the new posh housing development ('Olde Stonehouse Court') and small metalled lane, going directly over the M61 – the quietness of lane contrasting with the motorway roar.

7 – 1

At T-jn, TL, now running parallel to M61, to T-jn at the Bay Horse. TL (SP Rivington, etc.). Over M61 and immediately TL into Nickleton Brow, leading to Nick Hilton's Lane, then Dill Hall Brow, and along to the tempting Yew Tree. SO, on Knowsley Lane, (SP Anglezarke, etc.). Over reservoir to its far side, and as road bends, TR into BW (SP). Superb track up incline and alongside the high bank of another reservoir. TR at crest, going between bank and stone wall, to metalled lane. Exit over a step, TR along semi-metalled lane and gently down to T-jn with lane at end of BW. TL (at Rivington Village Club) and after 100m TR into BW (SP) at the old Rivington School. SO, lake nearby, following the track thro' trees and leading naturally back to the Great Barn. Magnificent!

Bridleway entering Lantern Pike, en-route for Rowarth and Mellor Moor (route 2)

On Winter Hill, near Rivington Pike and the unmistakable Pigeon Tower, looking west over Rivington and Anglezarke Reservoirs (route 3)

**Above Anglezarke Reservoir, impressive hill-climbing during the 2002
Commonwealth Games (route 4)**

Starting the bridleway traverse of Kerridge Hill, New Years day outing (route 7)

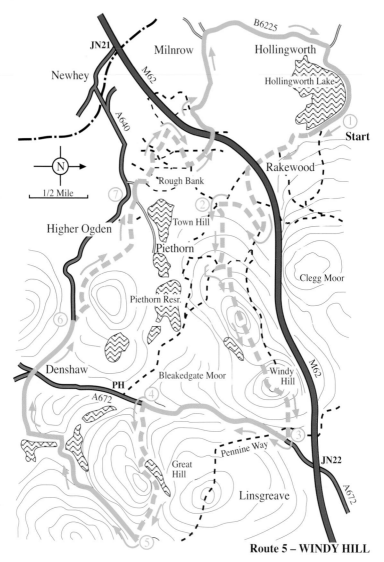

Route 5 – WINDY HILL

Route 5   **Windy Hill**

Off-road:	40%
Distance:	18mls.
Height gain:	1650 feet
Time:	$3^1/2$hrs.
Grade:	Difficult (-)
Rating:	***
Refreshments:	Visitor Centre (café) at start, pubs around route (see text).
Railway :	Littleborough or Milnrow, $^3/_4$ml or $1^1/_2$ml
Start:	Hollingworth Lake, Visitor Centre, Littleborough, Gtr. M/Cr. GR: 939153
Map:	LR 109 (Manchester); OL 21 (South Pennines), 1:25 000

Summary:
A fine route, given fair conditions – as good as any hereabouts. An array of hill tracks, including some excellent examples of gritstone pavé. Situations overlooking the huge Rakewood Viaduct to Hollingworth, and the long ascent of Windy Hill, are tremendous if good weather prevails (and best avoided if not). Great biking.

Route:
1 – 2
From the Visitors Centre TL, around the lakeside and towards the impressive viaduct carrying the M62 to Yorkshire, the highest road of its ilk in England. SO, the lane becoming gravel, under the viaduct, SO past Fm buildings, good dirt track alongside stream. SO thro' wide BW gate. Excellent track uphill to track crossing, (note SP 'FP only – no bikes', ahead). TR (acute) here, rising gently across hillside. SO thro' gate and up the fine packhorse trial, all rideable, SO main track – superb views – to gate and BW crossing.

North Midlands Mountain Bike Guide – Manchester, Windy Hill

2 – 3

TL, following good BW, level ground to T-jn (BW) where TL (acute), and thro' gate, following BW betwixt drystone wall and the hill. BW becomes potentially muddy holloway, circumvented on an exciting line several feet above the mire, hard by the wall. SO, variety of surfaces, absorbing riding, over a hillock which reveals the great mast – the high point of route. Last rise is across open country, likely to invoke a short push/carry. SO, around L of mast, then 200m metalled track to the road, just into Yorkshire.

3 – 4

TR, past carpark (Saddleworth Moor), shortly crossing Pennine Way (FP), and swiftly downhill until 200m before pub TL into obvious BW (no SP).

4 – 5

Thro' gate, easily down good broad track, thro' gate and along to cross the head of reservoir – quiet spot, hidden in fold of hills. Follow track around, leaving reservoir by smaller track, rideable up and over the moor to gravel track leading down to exit at next gate and road – super going.

5 – 6

TR, zooming delightfully downhill, around the bends (minuscule Tour de France?). Down to Junction (almost possible *sans* pedalling). SO at X-Rds (lights) at Junction Inn. Along Rochdale Rd., steady uphill, until $^3/_4$ml from Junction TR up track by 'La Pergoda' restaurant.

6 – 7

Follow BW SP (easily missed), the tarmac track becomes unmade and rough surface, increasingly hard work, steadily uphill, past Fm to T-jn. TL, gently rising gravel track, fine views. T-jn, TR, towards pylons and SO down the magnificent stony and walled track (watch the last bit). SO, tarmac, thro' pleasant hamlet (house 'Shippam 1710'), and steeply down to the bottom, Bulls Head and T-jn.

7 – 8

TL, nearly to main Rd, TR hard by PW Greenhalgh factory, metalled track. Fork L, behind factory, steeply up the cobbled walled track, rideable all the way with determination. SO, following main track zig-zagging up then over the rise, past Fms. SO, down the fine little walled track, interesting riding, gently down to T-jn of BWs. TR up rising, enclosed track, rideable to Carr's Fm. SO to T-jn of BWs (latter should be possible to ride for super-fit). TL, down superb BW, stony and walled to soon reach Fm and metalled lane over M62.

8 – 1

SO, downhill past golf course, to The Gallows (pub). TR, (SP 'Littleborough, Hollingworth Country Park'). SO, easy roadwork, to T-jn, TR (SP 'Hollingworth Lake'). Around the lake, (refreshments aplenty), to T-jn.at The Fisherman's Inn, TR. Continue around lake and in 100m TL into the Visitors Centre. Excellent outing.

High moorland, bridleway en-route for Windy Hill summit (route 5)

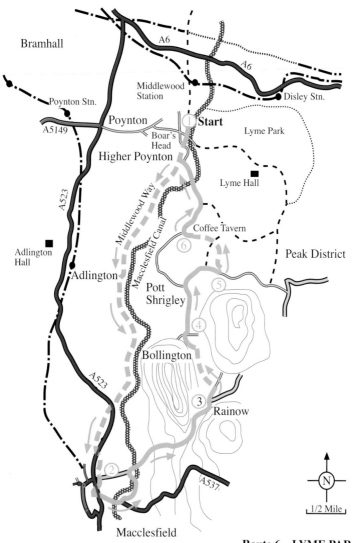

Route 6 – LYME PARK

Route 6	**Lyme Park**

Distance:	16^1/$_2$mls.
Off-road:	61%
Height gain:	1050ft.
Time:	2^3/$_4$hrs.
Grade:	Moderate
Rating:	** (W)
Refreshments:	Superb. Boars Head and cafe, Higher Poynton; many pubs in Bollington, Macclesfield and Rainow; Country Café and Coffee Tavern, Pott Shrigley (a must).
Railway :	Poynton, 1^1/$_2$ml. from start. Passes Macclesfield Stn.
Start:	Middlewood Way, Nelson Pit Visitor Centre carpark, Higher Poynton. GR: 934 844
Map:	LR 109 (Manchester); LR 118 (Stoke on Trent); Dark Peak / White Peak 1:25 000.

Summary:

A good introductory route, with part of the excellent Middlewood Way, some fine terrain close to Macclesfield, and return thro' a hilly Lyme Park.

Route:

1 – 2

From the visitor centre, drop down to the Middlewood Way and follow it pleasantly towards Macclesfield, over the viaduct at Bollington (views of the White Nancy, Kerridge Hill), across roads and past Tesco (café included). SO to lights, R and L, following stream and under railway, to exit finally at the junction before Macclesfield Stn., (Nag's Head on R).

2 – 3

TL, Care! SP Buxton Rd, A537, and under the bridge to lights. SO, steady rise on Buxton Rd out of town. Past Puss-in-Boots, over canal, TL into

Barracks Ln. At T-jn, along Higher Fence Rd, past pond, along track. SO, over canal to metalled lane, down to T-jn with Hurstfield Rd.

3 – 4

TR, along Hurstfield Rd, towards Rainow. SO uphill to Rainow (past pubs) and impressive Rainow Church. At fork TL into Chapel Ln, continuing as Stocks Ln to T-jn. TL (behind The Robin Hood), following splendid SP 'Bridlepath Bollington – fork L in 400yds'.

4 – 5

Following the SP, TL at the bottom, up gritstone-walled BW. Great views L of Kerridge Hill, as follow Gritstone Trail over rise and down to metalled lane, past cottages to exit Oakenbank Ln at jn.

5 – 6

SO, SP 'Pott Shrigley 1'. SO for 20m to follow Spurley Ln. Past Country Café, to jn, TR at Pott Shrigley. At Pott Shrigley jn along Bakestonedale Rd, (SP Kettleshulme 3, etc.). SO, past rural old brickworks trading estate. 200m beyond, TL (BW), space for several cars on otherwise narrow ln.

6 – 7

TL thro' gate, on track hard by the fence, after 20m TR, steeply up bank (BW SP). Follow small but sufficient line uphill, fine gritstone country, to run alongside the fence atop the hill, a good push, following the fence for 100m to gateway at L corner of field. Follow BW SP downhill - 50m from fence, to broken wall and tree with BW SP to next SP in 20m. Then down hillside for 300m to the gritstone-walled track that leads as BW down the stony track to the tastefully re-developed buildings of Birchencliff Farm. SO, down metalled BW to T-jn at bottom (beware speed bumps!).

7 – 1

TR, and immediately past The Coffee Tavern, up then downhill on small lane past West Parkgate and under aqueduct tunnel (CARE), to reach the Coppice carpark at sharp bend, and re-entry of Middlewood Way. SO, to reach the start in ¹/₂ml. A fine little route!

Above the steep rise: bridleway to Bakestonedale Quarry and Lyme Park (route 6)

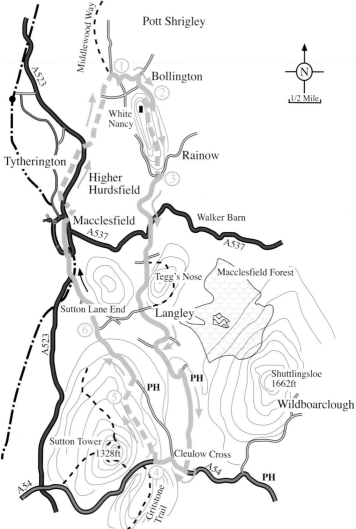

Route 7 – KERRIDGE HILL

Route 7   **Kerridge Hill**

Distance:	22¹/₂mls.
Off-road:	32%
Height gain:	1150feet
Time:	3¹/₂hrs.
Grade:	Difficult (+)
Rating:	**
Refreshments:	Bollington and Macclesfield cafés, many pubs around route (see text).
Railway :	Macclesfield station, ¹/₄ml from Middlewood Way, 2¹/₂ml from start.
Start:	Middlewood Way, Bollington viaduct carpark. GR: 931781
Map:	LR 118 (Stoke on Trent); White Peak 1:25 000 (except last stage).

Summary:

Interesting town and country; the easy Middlewood Way contrasts sharply with the tough cross country on often soft or ill-defined bridleways around Kerridge Hill and Sutton Tower. This is a reasonably demanding route, best after a dry spell, requiring a determined approach and a little experience to appreciate its charms.

Route:

1 – 2

TR out of the carpark, then 100m to T-jn at The Dog & Partridge. TL, along Wellington St., becoming Palmerston St. Under aquaduct, SO at lights, past Spinners Arms, to X-rds and New Conservative Club marking end of town. TR, down Church St, to T-jn (ahead, atop Kerridge Hill, is the curious White Nancy).

2 – 3

TL, at Church Inn (start for the tough little Kerridge Hill Fell Race). Follow lane, past new housing, then old industrial buildings, and TR.

Up the metalled track **pushing** to the top as this is **footpath status –** useful energy conservation! At Fm, TL, thro BW gate, (BW SP). Follow alongside hedge for 100m, thro' gate, jig thro' next, good BW SPs. Breaking out to more open country, traversing at mid-height across the long ridge of Kerridge Hill. Way-finding at a premium, heading towards the Fm, (whilst avoiding too-soft ground). At gate before Fm, (BW SP), keep R of trees and SO to next BW gate. Brilliant views over Rainow. Although the Gritstone Trail trends L and down, keep R, alongside wall up to gate with BW SP, in 100m. SO, to Fm, then steeply down last 50m to rd. N.B. latter section can be excruciatingly muddy in wet weather – OK if dry or frozen.

3 – 4

Exit the track as Lidgetts Lane to T-jn with rd. TR, along for 100m (11% hill begins), TL into small lane, steeply up. At jn, TL, then TR, leading up to main rd. (A537) crossing. SO, across and up tiny Back Eddisbury Rd. Over rise and down to T-jn. TL, then immediately TR, and steeply down to Langley and T-jn. TL, along 50m and fork R at church, up Cockhall Lane. SO, uphill to T-jn, exiting Back Hill Hollow. TL engaging on the long haul, (shared with route 23 out) past SP 'Higher Sutton, 2000' and the Gritstone Trail to T-jn. TR, following principal road (and Cheshire Cycleway). SO past the Hanging Gate (enticing), now with fine views R to ridge, topped by Sutton Tower. SO, steadily rising yet again, (Shutlingsloe, 508m on L). SO to crest and quickly down to X-rds. TR, along A54 (SP Congleton), downhill. Beyond the bottom, rise for 50m and TR into the broad BW (SP) – route 23 (out) continues to Winkle Minn.

4 – 5

Now for the tricky bit! Continue for 200m until just before Fm and TL thro' gate, following track across field (no SP!). Across grass, to gate in 150m. SO, same direction, unmarked, faint line across grass. Gently down across tiny stream (no SP) to crest rise in 75m – BW gate and SP now visible. SO, following BW SP, thro' small metal gate, towards next Fm, 150m. Gently down, potentially muddy. Exit field via BW gate. TL (BW SP) along short lane, then TR between houses to BW gate (SP).

SO, following SP to next BW gate at bottom R of bumpy field. Lift over mud preferable, SO in line of BW SP, trending down toward stream on R. Along general line of stream, skill required to avoid too-soft ground, to continue SO thro' next BW gate (SP). SO, 50m thro' next BW gate, bottom of hill. SO, around L of pond. Final 100m is heavy going, traversing leftwards up across bank (carry?) to thankfully exit onto the good Fm track, via gate.

5 – 6

TR, easily down track, (BW SPs) and SO some way, pleasantly, to T-jn with rd. TL, (opposite is Lower House Fm). SO to Sutton Lane Ends.

6 – 1

SO to T-jn and TL, under canal (at James Brindley's house) to T-jn with A523 (Macc – Leek). TR to Macc, then fork L at lights to town centre. TR at lights, SO to Stn., SO, under bridge to Middlewood Way (SP). Follow across rd, behind Tesco (café), to continue towards Marple on the Middlewood Way, as it winds under, alongside then over the Silk Rd. to reach the old railway track, heading towards Higher Poynton. At Bollington viaduct, descend steeply to the start, immediately below.

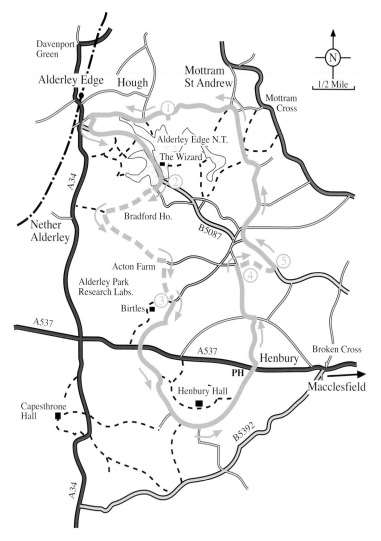

Route 8 – ALDERLEY EDGE

Route 8   **Alderley Edge**

Distance:	13½mls.
Off-road:	24%
Height gain:	450 feet
Time:	2½hrs.
Grade:	Moderate
Rating:	* (W)
Refreshments:	Café and pubs in Alderley Edge, mobile snacks normally at the Edge NT carpark. Tea shop on A537 at Henbury.
Railway :	Alderley Edge, ½ml. From start.
Start:	Alderley Edge National Trust carpark (below the Edge). GR:861783
Map:	LR 118 (Stoke-on-Trent).

Summary:

An easy introductory route, around interesting Cheshire countryside, although roadwork deceptively hilly. Tracks are good, a useful route when others are out of condition, apart from one short BW, easily avoided if wet. Fine woodlands, even if these often restrict views from the famous Edge. Good for a convivial, short outing.

Route:

1 – 2

The lower National Trust car park is an old quarry and lies well below the Edge on the lane from Alderley Edge to Mottram St.Andrew. TL out of here, downhill to Alderley - plenty of evidence of local sandstone in the vernacular building. At X-rds exit Moss Ln and TL, along Trafford Rd. Uphill for ½ml to T-jn and TL, steadily uphill, over the crest and past The Wizard. 100m past the top NT car park, TR into Bradford Ln.

2 – 3

SO to T-jn, TR (still Bradford Ln). Past the Wizard Caravan Park, now BW. SO, leaving tarmac for unsurfaced wide track through woodland. At T-jn, TL (BW) along Hocker Ln. SO to X-rds and TR (BW, SP) on good track. SO, easy going on long track thro' more open country (gates and cattle grids) to T-jn with Rd.

3 – 4

TR and past Over Alderley Church (fine architecture), then down to X-rds with main rd (A537). SO (care), SP 'Pexhill 2'. SO to T-jn and TL, circumventing the grand Henbury Hall, leading down to crossing of A537 (again). SO, (on L is Blacksmith's Arms, on R garden centre with excellent tea-shop). SO, along Potter St to T-jn in 100m. TL, and on to fork R along Andertons Ln. SO to T-jn and TL. SO for 100m and TR, downhill to minor ln crossing.

4 – 5

TR at Cross Ln, (BW) and past Fm. Initially good track, but beyond Fm can become **very** soft unless dry conditions. SO, down to stream and more pleasantly up to meet road crossing (B5087).

NB. *The BW is easily avoided by continuing SO past Cross Ln, exiting Wrigley Ln at T-jn, TR. SO to four-way jn, TR and in 100m TL (where the original route arrives from opposite direction).*

5 – 1

Exiting the BW, TL along B5087, and TR (SP 'Mottram St Andrews 1^1/$_2$'). SO, on Oak Rd, to T-jn. TL, along Priest Ln. Into Mottram (fine sign - village origins 1086). SO, along Alderley Rd to the start. A pleasant little route, enjoyable in all the seasons – even possible (exciting) in arctic conditions after heavy snowfall.

Approaching Nether Alderley in (rare!) arctic conditions (route 8)

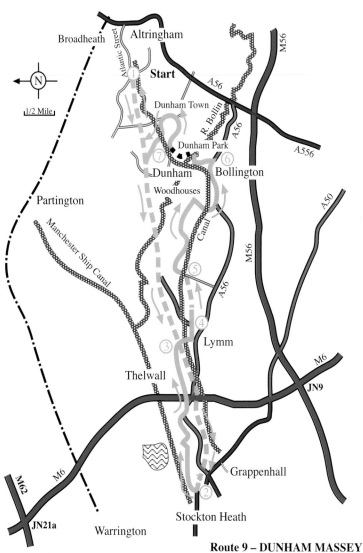

Route 9 – DUNHAM MASSEY

Route 9   **Dunham Massey**

Distance: 20mls.
Off-road: 55%
Height gain: 150 feet
Time: $2^3/4$hrs.
Grade: Moderate
Rating: * (W)
Refreshments: Lymm – café, chippy and pubs, several pubs
                   around route (see text).
Railway :   Altringham (Navigation Rd station),1ml
Start: Trans Pennine Trail, Atlantic St carpark,
                   Broadheath, Altringham. GR: 751888
Map: LR 109 (Manchester).

Summary:

An easy route, taking the Trans Pennine Trail (disused railway track), between Altringham and Warrington. Crosses the canal at the interesting old market town of Lymm (a good stop), returning mainly on small country lanes and BW thro' the parkland of Dunham Massey mansion. Short BW from Lymm (usually delightful) can be avoided if wet, otherwise all-season route, (tested on veteran cycle, at night, in winter!).

Route:

1 – 2

From carpark (free) TL, along Trans Pennine Trail going west. SO, good track past various crossings and bridges, including the Railway Inn and 'Bikes of Lymm' – handy shop! Past the Ranger Centre (info and maps) and its curious sculpture. SO, under M6 and back of housing as reach outskirts of Warrington. Short descent by sandstone bridge to T-jn with rd, exiting Trans Pennine Trail (track).

2 – 3

TR, along Bradshaw Ln, to T-jn in 200m. TR, following the wide Manchester Ship Canal, Thelwall New Rd. SO, past school and sandstone church to the Pickering Arms and old Post Office in picturesque Thelwall village. SO to TL at stone cross, into Lymm Rd to T-jn with A56. TL, along for 150m and TL (SP 'Statham $^3/_4$'). SO under the towering Thelwall Viaduct (M6), on quiet wooded lane. SO, over crossing, along Whitbarrow Rd, to cross the Trans Pennine Trail, (could return from here).

3 – 4

SO, past The Balmoral and up short rise (few gradients on this route!), SO at X-rds, under canal and into the centre of Lymm. Down to T-jn (at Spread Eagle) and TL. Follow Eagle Brow around bends and pond to Lymm Cross and stocks. TR immediately, Pepper St.

4 – 5

SO, cobbled / tarmac, past school, directly into BW (SP 'Oughtington 1km'). Superb track, thro' trees and alongside canal, to last 50m worthy of lift over soft ground. Exit BW and TL onto Oughtington Ln. (Note – could avoid above BW by TR immediately before it, then TL into Oughtington Ln).

5 – 6

Over narrow canal bridge, along Oughtington Cres. SO, becoming Stage Ln, to lights, going SO – single track as Spring Ln. SO, to eventually cross the canal, and immediate TL, leading to T-jn with A56. TL, (using the small service lane avoids some of the potentially busy A56), and continuing past Ye Olde Number Three to TL at The Stamford Arms, along Park Ln. (Note – if busy, could make way along path off the A56).

6 – 7

SO, past The Swan with Two Nicks, (attractive stopping place) right to the end of the lane, and **push** over the ultra narrow footbridge, across the Bollin. SP 'Bollin Valley Way'. TL, following easily the metalled BW. Glorious track thro' the park, with fine views to the mansion of Dunham Massey, (usually open to the public).

7 – 1

Exiting the park, TR, and past the estate entrance, along Woodhouse Ln. TL, off major rd into Woodhouse Ln, towards Dunham Town (hamlet). SO, then take L fork at the church. SO, over canal to T-jn. TR to the

Trans Pennine Trail, crossing at The Railway Inn. TR and follow the Trail directly back to the start. Possibly the easiest (certainly least hilly) route, but nevertheless it has a certain charm – especially on a frosty and bright Sunday morning, off-season.

The Swan with Two Nicks just before Dunham Massey Park and Hall (route 9)

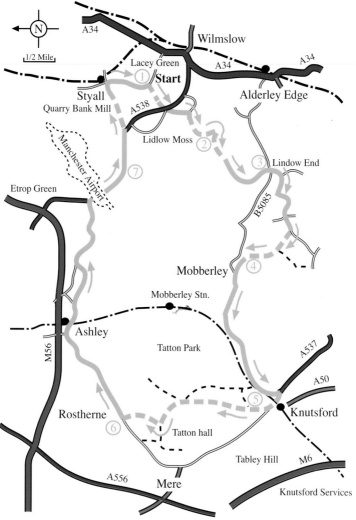

Route 10 – TATTON PARK

Route 10 **Tatton Park**

Distance:	21mls.
Off-road:	41%
Height gain:	300 feet
Time:	3^1/$_4$hrs.
Grade:	Moderate
Rating:	*
Refreshments:	Tatton Park (Stables Café); Penny Farthing Museum Coffee Shop, and many others in Knutsford; Quarry Bank Mill Café (Styal); plus several pubs, all directly en-route (see text).
Railway :	Wilmslow station,1ml from start. Knutsford, en-route.
Start:	River Bollin carpark, Lacey Green, Wilmslow; on B5166 (Wilmslow – Styal). GR: 840822.
Map:	LR 109 (Manchester) 118 (Stoke-on-Trent) Explorer 268 (Macclesfield), 1:25 000.

Summary:

Not a difficult route, but a fair length, so allow plenty of time for route-finding (and refreshment stops). BWs vary from luxuriously metalled track thro' the vast estate of Tatton Park to the other extreme of the short, almost invariably muddy Fm track to Styall Mill – brief carry appropriate. A good day in the country.

Route:

1 – 2

From the pleasant start, cross the river and up the delightful, if short, track that leads up past Wilmslow Rugby Club and into Kings Rd (start of the popular Wilmslow half marathon). SO, over the A538 (care), into track of Racecourse Rd. SO, good track, around Lindow Common, to

TR into Lindow Ln. Follow unmade track L past Racecourse Fm. SO, excellent BW thro' wood to jn at wooden step where TL. BW becomes metalled lane after 100m – delightful. SO, to housing, as Rotherwood Rd.

2 – 3

TR, along Moor Ln. Past Garden Centre (coffee shop), and in 100m (where rd swings R), continue SO into BW (SP). SO, easily followed track, to open ground, to large half-timbered barn. Follow metalled track L, and SO to ln and past The Plough & Flail. R at fork, under pylons and in 100m fork L at grass triangle. In 50m TL, and on to exit Paddock Hill Ln at X-rds of B5084.

3 – 4

SO, along Warford Ln. TR into Noah's Arc Ln, SO to T-jn. TR, then after 30m TL into Pedley House Ln. TR onto metalled BW (SP), toward Warford Grange Fm. Ignoring turn to Fm, continue SO, BW (SP), beside pond. Past barn and keep hard by fence on L, BW SPs. SO across grassy field (no track), keeping to L side. At far side, bend R, 20m, past stile, then SO at BW SP. Expansive views R, of Alderley Edge. Follow track R, thro' BW gate (SP) – minor mud at gate. Follow BW SP line (hopefully!) across open field, heading towards a constriction at the far corner, and thro' BW gate. SO, easily now between hedges, gently down to soft ground. Follow track, can hold water with ruts from 4-WDs. Improves as leaves low point and reach metalled lane.

4 – 5

The lane leads up to this pleasant backwater of Mobberley, at the Bulls Head. TL, and past The Roebuck, as road rises past Hillside Bird Oasis, to T-jn with B5085 (care). TL, along Town Ln. (*Note: if busy, some of the way to Knutsford can be made along the path*). SO, past Ilford Films (1903), now Knutsford Rd, into Knutsford. Keep R at fork, by The Builders' Arms, and quickly down to lights. TR, along Brook St, downhill 100m to T-jn. TR, under railway, King St – thro' the fascinating old centre of the town (one-way), with its Italianate buildings, hidden courtyards (including Penny Farthing café) and Gaskell Museum (the town featuring in the Victorian novelist's works).

5 – 6

Exiting King St, continue SO into track that leads thro' the impressive
gates and into Tatton Park. Free entry on foot, horseback or bike! SO,
past Tatton Mere, with Tatton Hall in distance, on other side. At T-jn,
TR, heading for 'Rosthorne Exit' (Stables café L here). SO to park exit,
pleasant riding, all metalled track.

6 – 7

TR, onto the long straight lane along the high perimeter wall of the park.
SO, past Ashley station to X-rds at The Greyhound. SO, along Back Ln.
Past school, TR into Back Lane, (ahead is Manchester airport). SO to
T-jn, exiting Back Ln. TR, past Magnolia Cottage and Trig point, then
zig-zag down (11%) hill, then up and SO to T-jn with A538. TR, (SP
'Wilmslow $1^3/_4$'), fortunately along the cycle path which shortly runs
under the airport runways, perfectly safely. SO to roundabout. Now have
to return to road, going SO and past the Moat House hotel.

7 – 1

SO, uphill (past rd on R, and R bend), to TL into BW, track but BW SP
is 50m from rd. SO at farm, on R of barn – likely to be rather a muddy
mess here. A short carry is sufficient to reach the fine enclosed sunken
track, overlooking the Bollin Valley. Nice track as descend to cross the
Bollin at Styal Mill. Steeply up cobbles to ln. TL (R is Mill café) and up
finally to exit at the B5166. TR, towards Wilmslow, along and downhill
to the start. An outing with a variety of tracks, fine country, good stopping places; but little hill-work, and care required on a couple of roads.

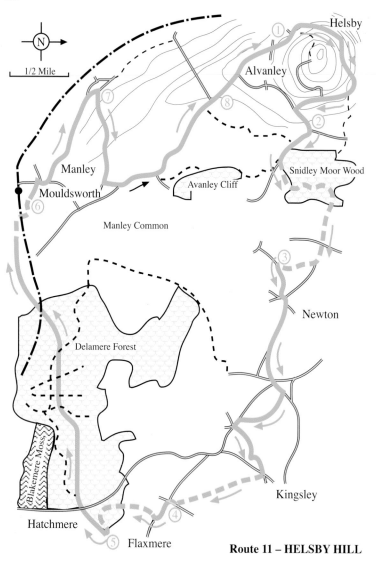

N

1/2 Mile

Helsby

Alvanley

Snidley Moor Wood

Manley

Mouldsworth

Avanley Cliff

Manley Common

Newton

Delamere Forest

Blakemere Moss

Kingsley

Hatchmere

Flaxmere

Route 11 – HELSBY HILL

Route 11	**Helsby Hill**

Distance:	16mls.
Off-road:	38%
Height gain:	500 feet
Time:	2^1/$_2$hrs.
Grade:	Moderate (+)
Rating:	*
Refreshments:	Several pubs around route, (see text).
Railway :	Helsby station (1ml from start).
Start:	Helsby Hill carpark, Avenley, Helsby. GR: 491749
Map:	LR 117 (Chester); Explorer 267 (Delamere Forest), 1:25 000

Summary:

An interesting area, including Helsby Hill (sandstone crags, site of Iron Age fort), Delamere Forest, and northern end of Mid-Cheshire ridge and Sandstone Trail. Tracks mostly very good, although the final BW is rather dubious and probably best avoided by the more sensible road return.

Route:

1 – 2

TL out of the secluded little carpark, nestling on the slopes of Helsby Hill – note that the summit is only accessible on-foot – certainly worth the effort. Follow the enclosed lane of Avenley Rd around the hill, sandstone much in evidence. SO, down onto Old Chester Rd. Keep R (L is No Entry), to X-rds. TR, Bates Ln heading away from the expansive views over the Dee estuary and its chemical complexes, to wooded land. SO, a mile to exit Bates Ln at T-jn. TL, Tarvin Rd, nice lanes. TR (SP 'Kingsley').

2 – 3

SO, along The Ridgeway, gentle rise to fork L into good track (SP 'BW to Shepherds Houses'). Delightful sandy track thro' woodland, SO past SP 'Snidley Moor, etc.' SO, following main track (SP 'Sandstone trail), rising to T-jn of tracks. TR, near edge of wood, over wooden steps, to exit Snidley Wood to open ground, easily followed track. SO, gates , SO across rd, on track to SP 'Waymarked path, Delamere Forest YH $3^1/_2$'. Steadily rising, but rideable, track to reservoir banking. Down to jn with rd. TR (still BW), following SP 'Eddisbury Way'. Down fine little hawthorne-hedged path to T-jn with rd.

3 – 4

TL, then take 2nd R, following SP 'Kingsley & Norley'. Up to high point - good views – down to TL at fork. SO to X-rds, exiting Meeting House Ln. SO (SP 'Croton $2^3/_4$') to TR into Depmore Ln. SO to T-jn and TL into Dark Ln. SO to T-jn and TR, then in 20m TL, immediately L of '3, Clifton House' into BW. Past BW SP, becoming delightful little enclosed track, just rideable. Gently rising sunken track to open ground, easily followed, hedge or barbed wire throughout. Exit at Fm, onto semi-metalled track, leading easily to T-jn with road.

4 – 5

TR, along 100m to X-rds and TL. SO to Fm and TR into BW (SP 'Hatchmere School Ln'). SO, BW SPs, to follow hard by R-side of field (hedge), clear track. SO, BW gate, to narrow track (BW SP) to cottages. Along semi-metalled enclosed track to BW crossing. TL (SP 'School Ln'), SO (BW SPs), to reach jn with rd in 200m.

5 – 6

Exiting BW, TR onto School Ln. SO for $^1/_4$ml to X-rds (sadly defunct café), SO along Ashton Rd – entering Delamere Forest. SO, past Sandstone Trail crossing at Barnesbridge – excellent picnic country. Exit Delamere under bridge, SO at X-rds (SP 'Tarvin, Mouldsworth'). SO (to where rd on L, SP Kelsall $2^1/_2$') and TR down track (no SP). Semi-metalled, in 100m becomes fine little track dropping down to cross the stream at small bridge. Nice track leads up, under railway bridge, 150m on to reach tarmac lane.

6 – 7

SO to exit Stable Ln at T-jn. TR, then TL (SP 'Leisure Drive'), immediately TR (SP 'Dunham Hill') on Chapel Ln. SO, (SP 'Dunham on the Hill 2$^{1}/_{2}$') at jn. SO, following Manley Ln. SO then TR up Quarry Ln, distant views to Welsh mountains. Exit Quarry Ln at T-jn, where TL. *(Note: Best to avoid last BW; TR here, following Sugar Ln to the B5393, where TL, directly – albeit some way – back to the start at Avenley).*

7 – 8

Only for the purist, prepared carefully to find the way across FP – best avoided. SO, shortly to hairpin bend, just to R of the apex of which go SO, open track to R of house. Follow gravel track (erroneous FP SP), branching R thro' wide gate, before pond. (Note – this BW route was posted here on official notice, dated 3/5/02). SO, along broad track for 20m to TL into original BW (not obvious), a good track behind Fm. Now, presented with three possible exits, but no SP. TR, thro' collapsing wide metal gate to follow fine, broad, ill-used (surprise!) track running down hard by L side of John's Wood. Nicely down, along line of telegraph poles, obvious way. Arrive at wet area around gate at bottom, which should **not** be permanently fixed … If it is, then legitimate to lift over – care! SO across open field, on line 100m from R-side, and down to dip, locating the obscure footbridge with difficulty. SO, lifting over stile, across stream, pushing up 50m across the rough grassy field (FP SP) to exit over stile. From here to rd, FP status, **push**. TL, thro' Abbotts Clough Fm, following semi-metalled track 200m, easily to T-jn with rd.

8 – 1

TR, uphill on Towers Lane (no SP), to T-jn. TL, past The White Lion, immediately after which fork L, along Helsby Rd. SO, past Clematis Cottage (1693). Views L over chemical works, R to Helsby Hill (wood). SO across X-rds, passing fine sandstone cottages – similar red colour and texture to the Staffordshire millstone grit of the Roaches, (route 14). And so back to the start.

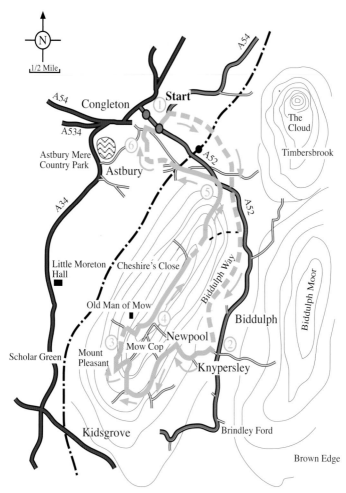

Route 12 – MOW COP

Route 12	**Mow Cop**
Distance:	14¹/₂mls.
Off-road:	44%
Height gain:	950 feet
Time:	3hrs.
Grade:	Moderate
Rating:	* (W)
Refreshments:	Congleton – cafés, chippy, pubs, etc. The 'Mow Cop' atop Mow Cop makes a good stop.
Railway :	Congleton, station (1ml from start, ¹/₂ml Biddulph Way).
Start:	Bidduph Way carpark, A54, ¹/₂ml N of Congleton centre. GR: 866634
Map:	LR 118 (Stoke-on-Trent)

Summary:

Surprisingly good value; pleasant, easy riding on Biddulph Way (from a rather uninspiring start), strenuous road hills (1-in-4) to Mow Cop ridge. Superb lane down to fine gritstone track and rapid road descent to BW entry to Congleton. Latter BW easy and pleasant (bone dry) in summer – but with two-foot-deep freezing water in midwinter! Old Congleton has interesting architecture, including original Ye Olde Kings Arms (circa 1535!), en-route.

Route:

1 – 2

From the inauspicious start to the Biddulph Trail, things should improve, and they rapidly do, once into the country. SO along the flat trail, alongside the River Dane, thro' gates, bridges and across lanes, pleasant country. Eventually under the bridge, track leading up to Newpool Rd, (trail terminates here).

2 – 3

TL along Newpool Rd, over trail, SO uphill to T-jn. TR, Tower Hill Rd (SP 'Mow Cop 1¹/₄'). Uphill to X-rds and TL, Biddulph Rd. SO to T-jn,

Leisurley riding in Tatton Park, from Tatton Hall to Knutsford – best expored by bike (route 10)

Snidley Wood, near Helsby Hill – pleasant tracks in sandstone country (route 11)

On the fine moorland bridleway, leaving The Cat and Fiddle (route 15)

The Mainwaring Arms in Hanbury, approx 12 miles from the start (route 16)

TL, Sands Rd. Past Nags Head to jn, and TR down Harriseahead Ln to T-jn. TR along Alderhay Ln. Steadily uphill to T-jn, exiting Dales Green Rd. TL, fast downhill to Chapel St. At Mt Pleasant Post Office, TR up Clare St (22% hill). Fine Staffordshire Moorlands village and country.

3 – 4

Immediately after Woodcocks Well School, SO along BW, SP 'Halls Rd', (as rd bends R). Great views over Cheshire plain. At fork, take L, gently down grassy track to the rd. TR, steeply uphill. SO, past the Cheshire View, to 25% gradient – stiff going! Up to T-jn, exiting Top Station Rd. TL, and past the castle folly of Mow Cop. At the end of High St, T-jn, TR along Wood St. Uphill again, past SP 'Old Man of Mow' remarkable gritstone pinnacle, nearby. Over the top (alt. 1099ft), steeply down Castle Rd to T-jn, at the Mow Cop Inn – worthy resting place.

4 – 5

TL, running along the ridge, affording views alternating between the Cheshire plain and Staffordshire Moorlands, along Mow Ln. SO, gently down. SO, up the sandy BW, SP 'Staffordshire Way', (where the rd descends L). FP SP, should read BW. Superb little track, over rise and nicely down to meet rd at T-jn. TL, SP 'Mossley 1¼', and quickly down fine ln, past Congleton Edge Methodist Chapel, (TR would return to Biddulph Way, via BW). SO down to TL into Boundary Ln, (immediately before the A52).

5 – 6

SO to T-jn, exiting Boundary Ln. TL, Leek Rd. Over bridge, past The Moss and directly TL into Astbury Lane Ends, then TR, Lamberts Ln – heading for the water tower. SO, then after row of cottages TR into BW, SP 'Lamberts Ln'. SO, over canal, good wide track. 50m before the gate, TR, (BW SP), across open field (no track). On far side of field, 50m from L edge exit thro' BW gate. SO, along fine little enclosed path. SO and out to the road. Note – in summer this is a delightful and dry path, but in winter it has flooded to a depth of two feet!

6 – 1

At rd, TL. SO along Howie Ln, into Congleton old town. TR, Chapel St. SO, past the Forrester's Arms, the fine church and plaque *'The Cockshoots*

– from Anglo-Saxon Cocc-Sceotas, the place where birds were trapped'. At end of Chapel St, T-jn. TL, to Town Hall in 20m (imposing Victoriana) at T-jn. TR, towards Tourist Info, and past Ye Olde Kings Arms (16[th]C). SO, plenty of refreshments, and Deans Cycles, to lights, (A523 crossing). SO, past Post Office as ln peters out at the bridge over the track (Biddulph Trail). TR, easily down to meet the trail. TL, retracing trail back shortly to the start. Apart from last BW, a good all-weather route, with some testing tarmac gradients providing stiff exercise!

The curious mock-ruin at Mow Cop, a landmark visible for miles around (route 12)

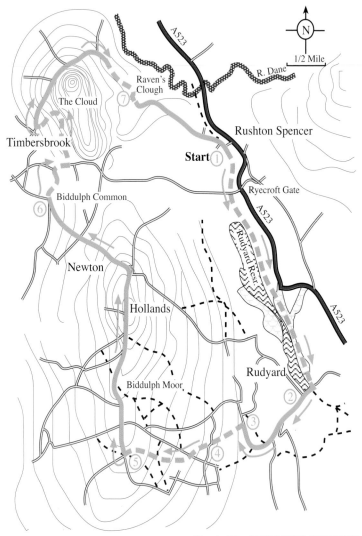

Route 13 – RUSHTON SPENCER

Route 13   **Rushton Spencer**

Distance:	16mls.
Off-road:	47%
Height gain:	1100 feet
Time:	2$\frac{1}{2}$hrs.
Grade:	Moderate (+)
Rating:	**
Refreshments:	Café and pub at Rudyard, Knot Inn at start, couple of pubs around route, (see text).
Railway :	None close - nearest is Congleton.
Start:	Rushton Spencer, small carpark behind Knot Inn, on Gritstone Trail. GR: 937625
Map:	LR 118 (Stoke-on-Trent)

Summary:

Some pleasant situations – around Rudyard and its lake, (so enjoyed by the Kipling family that they named their famous son after it), and up to the ridge of Biddulph Moor – a twin of the route from Mow Cop. Generally straightforward BWs, apart from short muddy section approaching the ridge. Fine going around Bosley Cloud, (Staffordshire's unique appendage for hill) completes a nice little outing from this trio around the Roaches. Best in reasonable weather.

Route:

1 – 2

From the secluded carpark, TR, heading along the excellent trail for Rudyard Lake. SO, and along the L of the reservoir. SO for $\frac{1}{2}$ml beyond reservoir, to the Rudyard carpark, and TL on tarmac track to rd. TL and under bridge, towards Rushton, up to T-jn. (Shared with route 23,out).

2 – 3

TL, along Dunwood Ln. Nicely downhill, glorious countryside, with 'Roaches gritstone' buildings. Keep R at fork, (route 23 departs L). Continue for $\frac{1}{2}$ ml and TR (SP 'Horton $\frac{3}{4}$'). Uphill $\frac{1}{2}$ ml (before reaching

Horton) and TL into BW (SP) at lone house, 'Tollgate Cottage'.

3 – 4

Heading across the valley, for ridge ahead – thro' gate in 20m, SO across field for 100m. Thro' gate, keeping on R of field, thro' BW gate. SO, keeping to L. Dry, if bumpy, in fair weather, SO down bank to stream crossing at bottom of field. Note: Cross via fine, small, bridge (BW) – avoiding the one 100m L (FP). SO, small track, to BW gate, (just R of tiny stream). SO, alongside hedge, on L of field. Reach good track in 100m. Thro' gate, glorious track alongside rocky stream. On for 100m to gate and ln, exiting BW. Super riding!

4 – 5

SO along ln 50m to apex of bend, SO into narrow track (remnants of BW SP?). Super little track, thro' holly-hedged enclosed way to cottages at rd, (SP 'Biddulph Moor 2', etc.). SO along rd for 30m, again at apex of bend, TR into BW. Thro' gate (SP disc missing!). SO, wide, rutted track. SO, main track – BW – and thro' gate, gaining height as surface deteriorates. SO, along L of field, pushing likely. Short carry preferred over some mud to reach the Fm on improving track. Steadily gaining height, beyond Fm, on good track, becoming metalled lane, past attractive cottage to exit the BW at X-rds.

5 – 6

TR, (SP 'Rushton $4^1/_2$',etc.). Past church and SO at X-rds, running along ridge, parallel with Mow Cop ridge, (on L). SO, (SP 'Rushton 4'). Terrific views! Past Trig. point (336m). After equestrian centre, follow rd L, Newtown Rd. Delightfully downhill, views R of Bosley Cloud, and beyond to Sutton tower, (above Macclesfield). SO at X-rds (SP 'Congleton'). Down to T-jn, exiting Common Rd. TR, along Overton Rd.

6 – 7

After 20m, TR, up fine gravel track (no SP). SO, over rise, to rd – Bosley Cloud ahead. TR, uphill on rd, and first TL to Fm. Superb track, although no SP, exiting Goosberryhole Ln, opposite Gritstone Trail. TR, on rd, around Bosley Cloud. SO, to exit Tunstall Ln at X-rds, going SO steeply down unmarked lane. TR at first lane, shortly past 'No Thro' Rd'

SP. SO, keeping R of Cloud House Fm. Downhill, past L bend and TR, steeply down the initially-metalled ln.

7 – 1

 The lane soon becomes unmade as it runs down delightfully to ford the stream, rising steeply to regain a tarmac surface (SP 'Unsuitable for motors') and on to T-jn. TL and shortly fine view toward Sutton tower. SO, SP 'Rushton 1$^1/_4$, Leek 6', continuing back to the start – another fine outing!

Bridleway after Bosley Cloud, fine Staffordshire-gritstone country (Route 13)

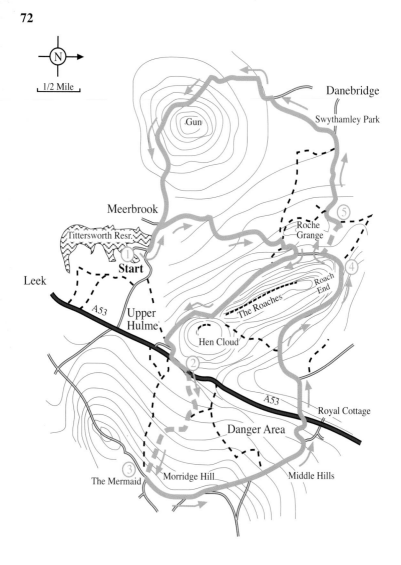

Route 14 – MORRIDGE HILL

Route 14	**Morridge Hill**

Distance:	18³/₄mls.
Off-road:	21%
Height gain:	2,350 feet
Time:	3 hrs.
Grade:	Moderate (+)
Rating:	*
Refreshments:	Reservoir café (recommended) at start, Tea Shop at Hen Cloud and Swythamley; pubs around route, including Rock Inn (Roaches favourite), and Mermaid Inn – third highest in England.
Railway :	None close – nearest is Buxton – a tough ride away.
Start:	Tittersworth Reservoir Visitor Centre carpark, Meerbrook, Leek, Staffs. GR: 994603
Map:	LR 118 (Stoke-on-Trent) and 119 (Buxton).

Summary:

Last in triumvirate around The Roaches – this time circumnavigating the famous outcrop and its prominent companion, Hen Cloud – providing arguably the finest gritstone climbs of the Peak. From the visitor centre small lanes gain most of the height to the Roaches, before crossing the Leek-Buxton rd. The BW all the way up to the Mermaid Inn provides most of the off-road interest – perhaps not very long, but good value, with unrivalled views of the Roaches skyline. The return, albeit almost all on metalled lanes, is nonetheless through some fine country and no pushover. YH in Meerbrook.

Route:
1 – 2

From the visitor centre, return to the rd and TL, over the reservoir to Meerbrook. TR at The Lazy Trout, keep R, following SP 'Roche Grange', steeply up to T-jn. TR (SP 'Upper Hulme 2, Leek 5'). Nice run down past the Roaches and Hen Cloud, magnificent views west – Tittersworth and Rudyard reservoirs, Bosley Cloud and Mow Cop. Down to Upper Hulme, to T-jn at bottom. TR, up to T-jn. TL, up past Ye Olde Rock Inn to the Leek-Buxton rd (A53), T-jn. TL, still rising, to TR (before crest) down clear track, with BW SP, but 20m down track. (Route 23, return, reverses the next section).

2 – 3

SO, BW SPs, gravel track down, thro' gate. SO to Swainsmoor Fm, thro' farmyard and thro gates to next – Little Swainsmoor – Fm. SO, beyond Fm on track along the line of telegraph poles and BW gate (SP). Track begins to peter out, make for L of barn ahead, and wooded cleft up the hillside. Glimpse Mermaid Inn on L skyline – distant objective. Thro' gate to L of barn (no track), following line parallel to and 50m R of telegraph poles. Steadily traverse field, to follow the fine, if indistinct, path down into the cleft (stone wall on L), to BW gate before fording stream (SPs). SO, following track up (a push). Follow general telegraph line as path expires, steadily uphill, to reach curious pair of BW gates, to track T-jn. TL, up the hill, SO, towards L fence, over grassy knoll, past beacon to the rd, at Mermaid Inn – a likely stop, if ever there was one!

3 – 4

TL, past the 'Mermaid of Blakemere', SO up rise past trig. point, following SP 'Royal Cottage 2¼'. SO across the fine, open high moorland rd and finally down to meet A53 at Royal Cottage, (X-rds). SO, SP 'Gradbach 2½', heading back towards the Roaches. TL at fork ('Corner House'). Down ln 200m, TR and past Hazel Barrow Kennels. Steadily rising traverse around Roaches massif, until the small ln reaches the col at T-jn.

4 – 5

TL, thro' gate in 50m, SO ¼ml, TR (acute) down good grassy track (SP 'Clough Head'). SO, thro' gate, nicely down, hard by wall on L, exiting thro' BW gate to metalled ln, (SP 'Roche End'). (Route 23 shares BW).

5 – 1

TL, down fine little ln, to T-jn. TL and to next T-jn. TL (SP 'Leek 5½').

Route 23 departs here. Thro' hamlet of Swythamley , SO, past 'Tea Shop', uphill to jn. TL (SP 'Meerbrook'). In 50m at X-rds, SO (SP Meerbrook). Stiff little rise – leading eventually to rapid descent free-wheeling to Meerbrook. SO (SP Blackshaw Moor $1^1/_4$'), and SO thro' Meerbrook, past YHA and Lazy Trout, to TR back into the Visitor Centre. Not a bad effort and situations – despite the preponderance of tarmac.

Ascending Morridge Moor to The Mermaid Inn, Hen Cloud in the distance (route 14)

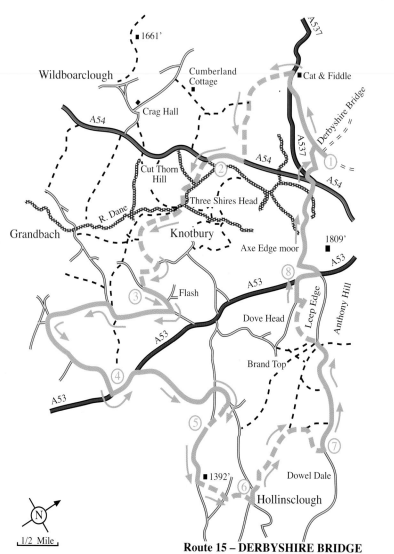

Route 15 – DERBYSHIRE BRIDGE

Route 15   **Derbyshire Bridge**

Distance:	21mls.
Off-road:	42%
Height gain:	2,750 feet
Time:	4$\frac{1}{2}$hrs.
Grade:	Difficult
Rating:	***
Refreshments:	Several remote pubs around route, with The Cat & Fiddle – second highest in England – near finish – or start!
Railway :	Nearest is Buxton – three (uphill) miles away.
Start:	Derbyshire Bridge carpark, at head of Goyt Valley, a mile from The Cat & Fiddle. GR:019716
Map:	LR 119 (Buxton); OL 24 (White Peak),1:25 000.

Summary:
A very fine route – incorporating some superb country and tracks as dip in and out of Dark Peak. Starting in Ches., visits Staffs. and Derbys. with BWs that are consistently of high standard – interesting, sometimes tricky, never too difficult – but their relative length and isolation demand a fair level of experience. A terrific outing!

Route:
1 – 2
SO from the carpark, uphill to T-jn with A537. TR, 200m to reach Cat & Fiddle and TL into BW across moors (SP). Excellent track, thro' Danebower Hollow, leads gently down to small quarry and exit gate to A54. TR, downhill $\frac{1}{2}$ml to TL into metalled track to Holt Fm.
2 – 3
Just before Fm, TR (BW) thro' wide gate and walled track. Into open field, TL, hard by wire fence on L of field. SO, sunken track, small white arrows, becoming clear as a track, by stream leading down to Pan-

niers' Pool – Three Shires Head. Across the famous packhorse bridge and TR. SO thro' valley, obvious stony track following infant River Dane. Thro' wide gate, L at fork, gently up fine little walled track. SO, rideable, around hill, past Fm, thro' gate. SO, (past 1st R), over rise and shortly TR (acute), down tiny but definite track. Absorbing riding, thro' gate, beside wood, down to ford the stream at bottom. SO, rising track, to eventually exit at Fm at the concrete track. Steeply up to reach ln at T-jn.

3 – 4

TL, continuing the gradient all the way to Flash (SP- 'Flash – highest village in England 1518ft' – no doubt!). SO, past the New Inn to T-jn at church. TR (SP 'Gradbach YHA'). Rapidly exchanging potential for kinetic energy, fly down a mile to bend and 1st TL, SP 'Goldsytch Moss'. Up to X-rds, TL. Steadily up, SO (ignore R), to T-jn with A53, at Morridge Top Fm – care!

4 – 5

TL, along A53, over rise, to fork R, SP 'Unsuitable Heavy Goods Vehicles'. Nice lane, ahead (distant) is Chrome Hill. A dip and steep little rise lead to T-jn. TR, then after 20m TL. Steeply down (SP 'Unsuitable for Motors') to the 'White House'. TR at Fm, into semi-metalled BW, (small BW SP). Good walled and grassy track – beware if wet. Past house, SO along improving ln to T-jn.

5 – 6

TL, past cottage (1787). SO, undulating until trig point (50m across field on L), and TL down unmade track (no SP). Delightfully down part-walled track to T-jn with rd. TR, then after 20m, TL, small ln past Fm. At acute bend, continue SO along track (no SP, but walled, obvious way). Quintessential mountain biking, mostly rideable, best gritsone! Emerge on semi-metalled ln to X-rds at Hollinsclough, by red 'phone box.

6 – 7

TL, and past chapel and 'VR' post box, steeply uphill to shortly reach BW. TR into walled BW start (SP). SO along same line, diagonally down across open field to small bridge, (FP crossing only). TL before bridge, to ford stream to TR 10m beyond far bank (SPs), and uphill on BW, more BW SPs. Up to wall (fine in dry conditions), TL, following SPs, thro' gorse, thin path, to semi-metalled track where TL (SP). SO, improving track, undulations, past cottage. Onwards and upwards, past Booth Fm to open metalled track that zig-zags stiff ascent to T-jn with the Dowel Dale – High Edge Raceway rd.

7 – 8

TL, good views, over two cattle-grids, SO (past Thelkeld Fm), to TL immediately after third cattle grid, into track. SO, gently rising, past cattle shed and then down to Fairthorn Fm. Ignoring obvious FP, TR (carefully!) across grass immediately in front of Fm on BW route to track and wide gate. Magnificent little grassy track follows above small ravine, thro' gates, to finally exit over bridge. SO along track, thro' gate to metalled ln. TR, steeply up to reach A53 (care).

8 – 1

TR, towards Buxton. Thankfully, after $^1/_4$ml TL (acute, no SP). Rises to open metalled rd across high moorland plateau of Axe Edge. Quickly across to T-jn. TL, along A54 and immediately TR for 100m to X-rd over A537 (Buxton – Macclesfied rd). SO, '16%' descent, delightfully easily to T-jn. TR, and directly back to start. Absolutely magnificent!

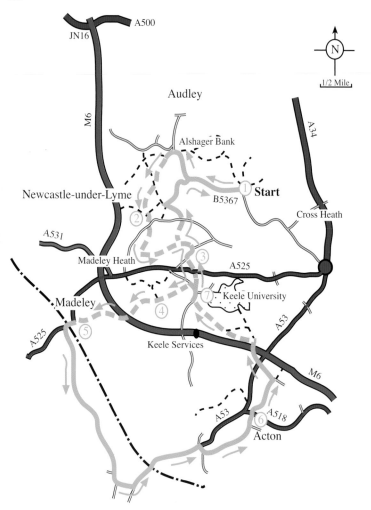

Route 16 – KEELE

Route 16	**Keele**

Distance:	20mls.
Off-road:	47%
Height gain:	750 feet
Time:	3hrs.
Grade:	Moderate (+)
Rating:	*
Refreshments:	Several pubs around route, including the fine village of Keele.
Railway :	Nearest is Stoke-on-Trent – 6mls.
Start:	Carpark/Picnic Site on B5367, Alsagers Bank, NW of Newcastle under Lyme. GR: 816479.
Map:	LR 118 (Stoke-on-Trent).

Summary:
Lowland travel through some pleasant Staffs countryside. Generally decent BWs, some open or rough grassy field crossings. Despite the lack of gradients, a not-to-be-underestimated outing as fairly long and route-finding skills helpful. Best in reasonable weather.

Route:
1 – 2
R out of carpark, to Alsagers Bank, along High St., SO past Greshley Arms. Downhill to Holmer End, past Post Office to TL before chippy, track, SP 'Podmore Ln'. SO along unmade ln until 100m before house ahead, TR into BW, via gate. Obvious track, picnic tables, horse-route marker posts. Gently down past the mere; pleasant, if unspectacular – setting the scene for route. SO, gates, 1ml to metalled track, gates, SO to T-jn.
2 – 3
TL, along 50m, TR at apex of bend, up unmade track beside cottages,

good path, to T-jn (tracks). TL (no SPs), past Fm and Cherry Cottage. Keep R at fork, down past 'The Meadows'. Hawthorne-hedged track, SO down past Hollywood Stables, pleasant woodland track to T-jn with rd.

3 – 4

TR, along $^1/_4$ml, to TL at 'Quarry Bank', metalled ln, SP 'No traffic except access'. Beyond houses becomes gravel track. SO, over A525 on fine little bridge, SO semi-metalled, past halls of residence (Keele Univ.), to exit Quarry Bank Rd at X-rds, in Keele. Sneyd Arms on corner. TR (Keele Rd), along 200m to TL, Highway Ln. Metalled ln, SO to 50m past sharp L corner, TR, thro' gate into BW (SP).

4 – 5

Along edge of grassy field, hard by wood to R. Bumpy, but rideable, to BW gate. SP, but lost pointer, diagonally L across open field of long grass. Better to follow track around field perimeter (R), until reach the diagonal line from gate to exit thro' BW gate at wire fence. Ahead, bottom of valley, runs M6. Follow SP across field of long grass, down to BW gate. TR – following SP 'public FP' (actually BW), keeping hard by hawthorn hedge to next BW gate (100m). TL and gently down, L side of field, SO over M6, following track R alongside M6, down stony track to gate. SO, 50m to metalled lane, past church and Old Vicarage to T-jn. Pleasant country.

5 – 6

TL, SO over railway, immediately TL, SP 'Baldwin's Gate 3, etc'. Alongside railway, to undulating country, past Manor Rd Private School, to X-rds. TL, SP 'Baldwin's Gate $^1/_2$ Stone 9'. SO $^1/_2$ml to T-jn. TL, SP 'Newcastle, A53'. SO, thro' Baldwin's Gate, past The Sheet Anchor, to X-rds at The Mainwaring Arms. TR, along Bent Ln. 100m, fork L, SP 'Acton'. Delightful sunken ln, stiff rise to Acton. SO, over main rd (staggered), SP 'Butterton $^1/_2$'. SO past hamlet to T-jn (opposite Park Lodge).

6 – 7

TL, continue SO over A53 (exiting Butterton Ln), along Lymes Rd. SO, semi-metalled track, BW. SO, under M6 to stony track, to R of M6. Easy track to exit Lymes Rd at T-jn with ln. Spire of Keele church on R.

7 – 1

TR, $^1/_2$ml to X-rds in Keele (with large yew). Exiting Three Mile Ln, SO along Quarry Bank Rd, returning along outward route. Past Sneyd Arms, over bridge to T-jn. TR, then TL into BW (after J.S.Cotton garage), no SP. SO, BW, up to Hollywood Riding School, to TR (leaving outward route), obvious track, steadily uphill, then quickly down to semi-metalled ln thro' Fm. SO to X-rds. SO, along Crackley Ln, SP 'Scot Hey $^1/_2$, etc.' SO, stiff rise, thro' Scot Hey, to T-jn at Alsager Bank. TR, exiting Scot Hey Rd, along Black Bank Rd. SO 200m to TL back into start.

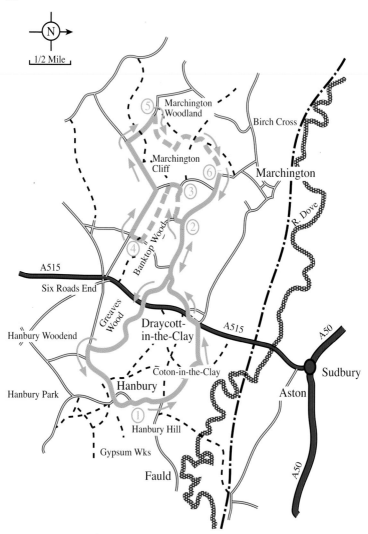

Route 17 – HANBURY HILL

Route 17	**Hanbury Hill**

Distance:	13mls.
Off-road:	23%
Height gain:	450 feet
Time:	2hrs.
Grade:	Moderate
Rating:	*
Refreshments:	Occasional pubs around route, including Cock Inn at Hanbury.
Railway :	Tutbury (3mls.).
Start:	Carpark/Picnic Site at Hanbury Hill, Hanbury, near the A515 and SE of Burton on Trent. GR:174283.
Map:	LR 128 (Burton-on-Trent).

Summary:

A short route, where dry conditions are required for an enjoyable outing, as there is one potentially sticky section. This is a charming little area, making use of the wooded escarpment that provides some limited sport thro' nice woodland. But beware the drainage cross-country, a clue from the nearby Draycott in the *Clay*! The Cock Inn, Hanbury, should be visited, from which can be found the traumatic episode of the country's largest explosion – a WW II underground conflagration of a high-explosive store and complete destruction of several farms – good job it was so isolated!

Route:

1 – 2

TR out of the car park and easily downhill to T-jn. TL, SP 'Coton-in-the-Clay, Draycott 1¹/₂'. SO to roundabout with A515. TL along Main Rd, SO for 150m and TR at the Roebuck Inn, along Toby's Hill. SO, over rise to T-jn. TR, along Stubby Ln, (A5017). Continue until R curve, where TL, up Woodedge Ln.

2 – 3

500m after jn, TR into the first BW (SP). SO past the white house, to a more enclosed track, into a mildly muddy stretch (pushable in good conditions – likely desperate in wet!). Gain metalled drive, to exit to T-jn, grass triangle.

3 – 4

TL, steeply up ln to top, and TL into BW, (SP). Magnificent (albeit short) track thro' wood (safely above the clay!), SO to exit BW at ln crossing.

4 – 5

TR, long straight, to bend, and TL, SP 'Hoar Cross'. SO, another straight rd, to TR at SP 'Marchington Woodlands 1¹/₂, Uttoxeter 5'. SO, partway downhill, to TR just before houses, into BW (SP).

5 – 6

BW begins as delightful, narrow woodland track. Now with short patches of light muddy going – can be circumvented with cunning if dry, but would resort to ploughing thro' in wet. SO, SP indicating FP – actually BW. Track fine again, to track jn, where TL, thro hedge and BW gate (SP), exiting wood. SO, boldly down the open field, bumpy, long grass but rideable – making for wide gate on far side. Thro' gate, keeping hard by R side of field, tracks. SO thro' next wide gate, and still on R side. 200m thro' another gate, SO to gate with BW SP. Continue on R, another gate and SP, keeping on R, yet another gate. SO (hopefully!), across field, hard work, but finally rd can be seen on far side. Heading for wide gates, two in 10m. Thro' these to rd. Exit BW to B5017.

6 – 1

TR, towards the wooded escarpment. SO, SP 'Draycott 1¹/₂, Burton 9³/₄', along Stubby Ln. SO, past Toby's Hill, to crossing of A515 (care!). SO, past St Augustine's Chapel, along Pipehay Ln. SO, past school, and down Greaves Ln. Up steep hill to exit Greaves Ln at T-jn. TL, along Wood Ln. SO, SP 'Hanbury 1, Tutbury 4'. SO to Hanbury, to T-jn. TL, SP 'Coton1, Tutbury 3'. Now at Hanbury Hill, useful pause at the Cock Inn, then down Hanbury Hill for ¹/₂ml, to TR back into start.

Near the finish – The Cock Inn, Hanbury (route 17)

The Fauld Explosion

AT 11 MINUTES PAST 11 ON THE MORNING OF NOVEMBER 27TH, 1944, THE MIDLANDS WAS SHAKEN BY THE BIGGEST EXPLOSION THIS COUNTRY HAS EVER KNOWN.

4,000 TONS OF BOMBS STORED 90 ft. DOWN IN THE OLD GYPSUM MINES IN THE AREA, BLEW UP, BLASTING OPEN A CRATER 400ft DEEP AND 3/4 MILE LONG.
BUILDINGS MANY MILES AWAY WERE DAMAGED.
THIS PUB HAD TO BE REBUILT AND ONE FARM, WITH ALL ITS BUILDINGS, WAGONS, HORSES, CATTLE AND 6 PEOPLE COMPLETELY DISAPPEARED.

YOU WILL FIND THE STORY OF THE EXPLOSION HERE AT THE..............

COCK INN

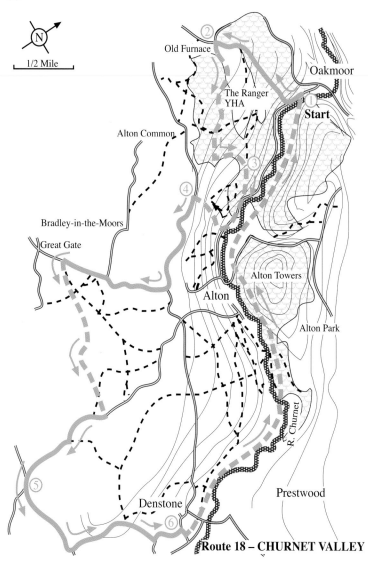

Route 18 – CHURNET VALLEY

Route 18	**Churnet Valley**

Distance:	16mls.
Off-road:	58%
Height gain:	750 feet
Time:	3hrs.
Grade:	Moderate (+)
Rating:	**
Refreshments:	Pubs at Oakamoor, café at BW near Alton, in heart of Churnet Valley. Pub at Denstone.
Railway :	None close – nearest Stoke-on-Trent.
Start:	Carpark/Picnic Site at Oakamoor, end of Churnet Valley trail. GR: 053445
Map:	LR 119 (Buxton); Explorer 259 (Derby), 1:25 000.

Summary:
Nearby is Alton Towers, and the Valley track shows how the region gained its appellation of 'Little Bavaria', with fine wooded hillsides and mock castles. YH near start, at Dimmingsdale. Generally good tracks (with one potentially tricky fields section), and fine scenery characterize this nice little route, in an interesting location.

Route:
1 – 2
From the carpark, TL and follow the ln into the Churnet Valley, away from Oakamoor and alongside the River Churnet. In ¹/₂ml take R fork, and steadily up the delightful sunken ln thro' woods. Over the crest (YH off L) and nicely downhill to Old Furnace.

2 – 3
TL (acute) at Old Furnace (hamlet) at SP 'Dimmingsdale, BW'. Fine track, gently down, R at fork, BW SP. Alongside pools, SO at branch, just L of lake and stream. Delightful. SO, past wooden bridge. Short stretch of soft ground (carry?), then OK again as narrow track leads to stone wall and small bridge. Continue between wall and bank, past

Dimmingsdale mill along fence to exit onto a large track making T-jn at Earls Rock.

3 – 4

TR, along good track, past lake to meet rd at large café 'Rambler's Retreat', (Dimmingsdale – Forestry commission). TR, off rd, hard by L side of café, rising track thro' wood (no SPs). TR at fork, by Humble Bee cottage, pushing up fine little enclosed track to top, flatter, past houses. SO, improving riding to metalled ln and end of BW (SP). SO to T-jn at Hansley Cross.

4 – 5

TL, to Gallows Green, fork R at grass triangle (commemorative stone 'Site of Alton gallows ... erected ... Alton castle in 12thC ...'). SO, nicely downhill, SP 'Great Gate 1', over stream, steeply uphill to crest, TL (BW, SP) into unmade ln. SO along ridge-top, alongside hawthorn hedge – open fields, no track. SO, thro' several gates, to enclosed track. Thro' yellow gate to large oak with BW SP, follow it L, 200m across ploughed field – past two trees to exit thro' BW gate, (150m from L side of field). *Alternative is to follow L edge of field to same exit – preferable, unless dry.* SO, grassy, open field, assisted by gentle descent, past Fm (BW SP), and along enclosed track, nicely down to metalled ln. TR exiting Nabb Ln at T-jn.

5 – 6

TL, down to houses, to TL at SP 'Stubwood & Denstone'. Along Stubwood Ln, TL first jn. Follow around L at small grass triangle, down thro' Denstone to Denstone Cross at T-jn, exiting Oak Rd. Opposite 'The Tavern'.

6 – 1

TR, then after 50m TL into Churnet Valley Trail (SP 'Staffordshire CC Trail'). SO, along full length of trail, fine country, half-hour return to start at Oakamoor.

Returning to Oakamoor on the Churnet Valley Trail – disused railway line with views of the Gothic Alton Castle, whilst Alton Towers is well-hidden (route 18)

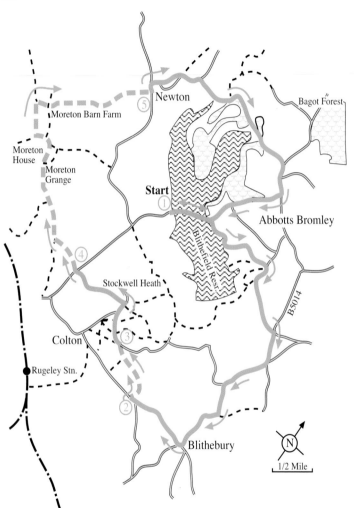

Route 19 – ABBOTTS BROMLEY

Route 19   **Abbot's Bromley**

Distance:	18mls.
Off-road:	30%
Height gain:	600 feet
Time:	3hrs.
Grade:	Moderate
Rating:	*
Refreshments:	Pubs around route (see text).
Railway :	Rugeley (3$\frac{1}{2}$mls.).
Start:	Carpark/Picnic Site at Blithfield Reservoir. GR:055236.
Map:	LR 128 (Derby & Burton-on-Trent).

Summary:

A fairly flat ride, but providing plenty of exercise finding and negotiating the field tracks thro' pleasant, if unspectacular country. Abbot's Bromley is noteworthy, indeed famous, for its traditional 'Horn Dance', performed annually for many centuries. Paths are across grassy fields or generally sound farm tracks, not to be underestimated. Could be combined with Hanbury Hill route (with transport between) for a good day out, given fair weather (and a stout constitution).

Route:

1 – 2

From the carpark on the south shore of Blithfield Reservoir head north, across the causeway. TR on its far side, along the north bank on tarmac track, past the picnic site. Continues as Port Ln to T-jn. TR, to X-rds, where TR. Bear R at next jn, over stream, along Newlands Ln. SO to 'Bear & Spectacles', where TR into Blithbury Rd. SO, finding BW on R, 150m after second rd on R.

2 – 3

TR into BW (SP), keeping along L of field, to wide gate. TL thro field and to R of copse (no SPs). SO, thro' next wide gate. SO (ignoring BW SP on stile), thro' copse, thin track, gently down to better going, hard by R fence. Pleasantly thro' oak copse, SO, thro' wide gate, past small pond and hard by R side of field. SO, another gate, to track enclosed by hedges, to metalled track and lane jn, BW SP (finally).

3 – 4

TL, along Newlands Ln. SO to Stockton Heath. At picturesque village pond, TL past Hamley Home Fm. SO to T-jn, TL and immediately TR into BW.

4 – 5

BW is tarmac initially, SP 'No Thro' Rd'. SO, over stream, past pylons, TR just before Lount Fm. SO, more wooded and muddy initially to cobbled-cum-grassy track, leading to wide gate and open field. SO to gate on far side, continuing SO thro' next gate. Note – SPs showing FP and BWs rather confused hereabouts. Continue around, to R of Fm, thro' gate and lane. SO, semi-metalled ln, to Fm. SO to track, at Farm End Cottage. SO, thro' wide, then BW gates, and hard by barbed wire on R, towards Moreton Grange. Across grass to decent track. TR at BW arrow, along line of overhead cables. After 100m TL, circumnavigating Fm on R, along concrete track. SO thro' gate, small BW SP, thro' Fm. Concrete becomes easy ride down gravel track, hawthorne hedges. At first track, TR (obvious path, but no SP). SO, $\frac{1}{2}$ml to Moreton Hall Fm. SO at Fm, track on L. Good track, down nicely to field. Follow ribbon of track on R, (150m from pylons). Thro' BW gate, hard by R of field. 50m, thro' BW gate near pylons (no SPs). Over small bridge, SO, L of field, (no path). 50m R of stile is gate, thro' this and next, and across field on track, to R of field. Emerge at top L corner of field, thro' gate to unmade lane. Gently up on improving surface to meet ln and T-jn at Newton Fm.

5 – 1

TL, along to fork and TR, SP 'Blithe $2\frac{1}{2}$, Kingston $3\frac{1}{2}$'. SO, to third on R. TR, SP 'Abbott's Bromley 3'. SO, views of Blithfield Reservoir, to

T-jn. TR, SP 'Rugely 6, B 5013'. SO, initial rise is rewarded by nice downhill rush over causeway to start. Watch out for punctures – the team garnered a record of repairs on this route!

Typical bridleway around Abbots Bromley – puncture alley in the spring! (route 19)

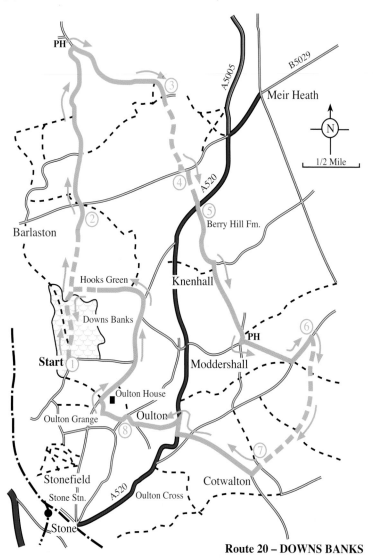

Route 20 – DOWNS BANKS

Route 20	**Downs Banks**

Distance:	13mls.
Off-road:	40%
Height gain:	750 feet
Time:	2¼hrs.
Grade:	Moderate
Rating:	** (W)
Refreshments:	Pubs around route (see text).
Railway :	Barlaston, (¾ml from route).
Start:	Carpark / Picnic Site at Downs Banks, (National Trust). GR: 901365
Map:	LR 127 (Stafford) and part LR 118 (Stoke-on-Trent).

Summary:

A fine little ride – the NT area of delightful woodland and banks that gives the route its name was bequeathed to the nation after WW II – a little gem on foot, horse or bike! All the BWs are enjoyable, and lanes visit some nice countryside, in this well-kept secret of rural north Midlands – within easy reach of the big conurbation of the Potteries. Worth searching out, particularly in spring when Downs Banks is carpeted in bluebells and frequented by wildlife. Nearby is Barlaston, Wedgewood Visitor Centre.

Route:

1 – 2

Continue along the track into Downs Banks, from the unobtrusive carpark; info board shows recent history and layout of the Banks. SO, passing several tracks off, thro' BW gate, on broad track to wide gate at

'Hooks Green'. TL, gently down glorious, unmade BW to semi-metalled lane. SO, past Fm to T-jn.

2 – 3

TL, on for 50m and TR. SO, SP 'Burton ³/₄'. SO, past Wedgewood Visitors Centre, to T-jn. TR, SP 'Cocknage 1¹/₄, Mere Heath 2¹/₂. Past Garden Centre (refreshments). SO, past phone box, steadily up to sharp L-bend, where TR into BW, at 'The Lodge'.

3 – 4

Nicely down, fine track, thro' wide gate at 'The Hollies', SO, thro' BW gate (SP). Keep hard by R fence. At next Fm continue BW, 50m from R of field. SO, grassy field, thin track now on L, by wire fence. Thro' last BW to rd.

4 – 5

TL along rd, and after 50m TR into next BW, SP, thankfully escaping rd. thro' BW gate. Around L of Gt. Hartwell Fm, following BW SP. Follow hedge on R, past posts to BW gate – exit to rd. Thro' hedge, across busy rd, SO into small ln, SP 'Knenhall ¹/₂, Uddershall 1¹/₂'.

5 – 6

Downhill, past picturesque Boar Inn with its splendid pond, to T-jn. TR, steeply uphill, then TL into Leese Ln. Superb lane, continuing upwards to finally emerge at T-jn. TL, gradient easing, past magnificent pitch of Modershall Cricket Club, to an obvious track on R, by relay tower.

6 – 7

TR into wide track, towards mast, but immediately TR, thro' BW gate, SP. Fine little track, whizz down, thro' wide gate, across track, SO thro' next wide gate. SO, down, barbed wire fences. SO, BW gate, rising, under pylons, wide gate, to wider unsurfaced track between hedges. Fast stony descent to Fm, and out to rd.

7 – 8

SO, ¹/₄ml down to T-jn. TR, continue to jn, TL and TR into rd SP 'No Thro' Rd' – short lane, the last 20m requiring a **push** as one-way leads to the T-jn with nasty main rd – care! Re-mounting, TR, thankfully escaping at TL after ¹/₂ml, SP 'Oulton', into Vanity Ln. Steeply up the delightful sunken ln, thro' sandstone cutting, to T-jn.

8 – 1

TR (exiting Vanity ln), 200m to T-jn, exiting Church Ln. TL, down past The Wheatsheaf, Oulton. 150m and TR, SO past Oulton House, up to T-jn. TR, SO past first ln, over rise to TL at next. Thro' 'S' bend, past 'Hook's Green'. SO into track as it it leads from ln, BW thro' gate back into Downs Banks, rejoining outward route. Thro' wide gate, delightfully down the track to the start – a fine little outing.

Bridleway through the glorious Downs Banks (route 20)

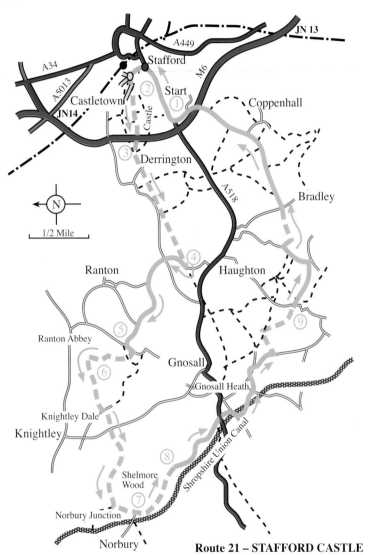

Route 21 – STAFFORD CASTLE

Route 21   **Stafford Castle**

Distance: 23mls.
Off-road: 52%
Height gain: 525 feet
Time: 3³/₄hrs.
Grade: Difficult(-)
Rating: *
Refreshments: Pubs around route (see text).
Railway :   Stafford Central Station (³/₄ml.).
Start: Carpark/Visitor Centre,
                     (Stafford Castle - ruins). GR: 903221
Map: LR 127 (Stafford)

Summary:

A relatively long outing, visiting some pleasant mid-Staffordshire countryside. Predominantly flat, some good cycle tracks are interspersed with rough-grassed fields, requiring some effort in route-finding – the grade more a reflection of this than terrain, providing a certain sense of satisfaction in its completion! Stafford Castle provides a unique aspect to an interesting day in the country – and is a fairly short drive from the previous route, Downs Banks, making quite a contrast if both are tackled on a full day.

Route:

1 – 2

From the pleasant castle visitor centre, return to the main road and TL, towards Stafford centre. SO at lights, to TL at roundabout, SP 'Castlefields', along Kingsway. TL at roundabout, along Redgrave Drive for 100m and L into estate. Follow gravel track thro' estate, gently rising behind houses to exit via BW gate.

2 – 3

SO, into fine enclosed track, continuing on rough grassy track at edge of ploughed field 50m from hedge. Stafford Castle on far L. SO, gates, hard by hawthorn hedge on R, towards Fm. SO, across field to BW gate, SO along semi-made track, bear L, BW SP. Keep hard by R fence, SO and exit via BW gate. Down concrete track, under M6, follow thin track, hard by hedge on R, to opening in field to BW SP. Across field 75m from L of field – nice. SO at far side, into enclosed track and footbridge, via BW gate to metalled ln.

3 – 4

TR into ln, then after 50m TL, (before railway bridge) up to cycle track – TL onto disused railway, to Gnosall. SO, SP 'The Red Lion', on fine unusually narrow track. SO, SP 'Newport 10'. At second bridge TL, into obvious carpark.

4 – 5

TL onto rd, over bridge, SO SP 'Ranton 1¾, Eccleshall 6'. SO, SP 'Ranton 1½'. TL at Bart's Fm. Up Butt Ln to T-jn, at 'Hand & Cleaver' and TL.

5 – 6

After 150m, TR into BW (SP). But instead of the obvious track to the Fm, at rd go thro' adjacent BW gate into field, hard by L, near Fm track. SO, to R of barn, thro' BW gate, then L behind Fm on track, past stables, SO, gate, SP, to field on L by hedge. SO, alongside wood, gate (SP). Alongside ploughed field, thro' wide gate – ahead is seen Ransom Abbey. SO, wide track, thro' BW gate, on 75m across field, exiting thro' BW gate to broad track to abbey.

6 – 7

TR, then directly TL, thro' BW gate on obvious track thro' wood, near field edge. SO, good track, thro' wide gate (SP), hawthorn hedges, to T-jn with rd. SO into BW track (no SP). SO, following main track, R side of field, bumpy, to far side. TR, BW SP, thro' BW gate and SO across ploughed field (rideable if dry, if not carry required). At far side is an indent and BW gate, beside pond. SO, delightful wooded track to cottage. At lane, TR then TL after 10m, metalled track past Knightly Hall. Thro' Fm, keeping R, on good track. SO, 200m to single-strand barbed wire across track. Unhook and continue SO, 75m to next BW gate, SO by fence, then across field, still track, BW SP, to gate at far side. SO, another BW gate, track, keeping L, to semi-metalled ln. Continue on L (ignore BW on R), to concrete track (still BW), and SO to end of BW at T-jn (Norbury Jn). Canal basin and pub.

7 – 8

TL, continuing to sharp R-bend, (before tunnel) and SO into BW (semi-hidden BW SP). SP 'Shelmore Trout Fishery'. SO, (ignoring track on R), to L of wood. Some soft ground, to concrete track. Bear R, to cottage and metalled ln, end of BW.

8 – 9

SO along ln, a mile to bridge under ex-railway, to X-rds at Gnosall. SO across A518 and along Mill Ln, down to T-jn. TR, just past Boat Inn. Over bridge (canal), TL, along Quarry Ln. Fine little ln becomes even finer unmade track, hawthorn hedges, past wet area to X-rds. SO across ln, track resumes, delightfully down to rd. TR, past Lower Reule Fm to TL into BW (SP), just before Sewerage Fm. SO, good track, to BW T-jn. TR (no SP). SO, main track. Easily to gate, then nettle-filled track, circumvented on L of hedge for 100m to resume original line. Variable track leads to metalled ln, BW end.

9 – 10

SO along ln for 150m, then TL, thro' ford (slippery!). TL into Alstone Ln, to Alstone Fm. TR into BW (SP), alongside Fm, SO thro' gate. Hard by barbed wire on R of field, to far side. Thro' BW gate, 10m from R side, immediately TL, hard by L of field – bumpy! SO, thro' BW gate, 200m across long-grassed field (BW SP), on line 50m L of large crater, to exit at BW gate and copse on far side. Thro' fine copse on track to rd crossing.

10 – 1

SO, along Furlong Ln to T-jn. TL, SP 'Coppenhall'. SO, over M6 and down to T-jn. TL, Sandown Rd. Thro' estate, castle now visible, down to main rd at traffic lights. TR (SP 'Castle Bank') along A518. Over rise and TL back into 'Castle Carpark' (SP) – not without effort!

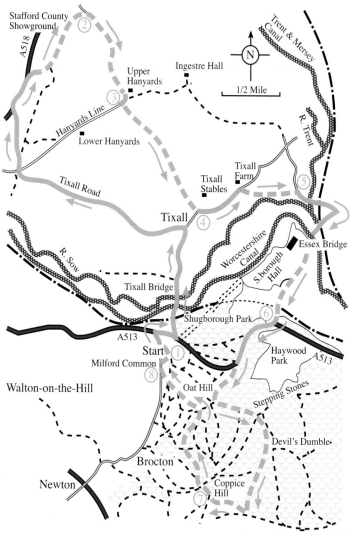

Route 22 – SHUGBOROUGH

Route 22   **Shugborough**

Distance: 15mls.
Off-road: 62%
Height gain: 650 feet
Time: 2¹/₂hrs.
Grade: Moderate(+)
Rating: *
Refreshments: Café and 'Barley Mow' at start, pubs around
                     route (see text).
Railway :   Stafford station 4mls.
Start: Carpark, Milford Common . GR: 972211
Map: LR 127 (Stafford); Explorer 6 (Cannock Chase)
                     1:25 000.

Summary:

A moderate outing, around the fine region immediately to the east of
Stafford, centred around Shugborough, stately home of the Earl of
Lichfield. A very fine foray into the northern aspect of Cannock Chase,
justifiably popular with generations on foot, by wheel and horseback –
there's plenty of room for all. Long may it be so!

Route:

1 – 2

From the fine carpark at Milford common, TR along the minor rd to   T-
jn with main rd at Barley Mow, and TR. After 75m fork L along The
Green, then in 150m to T-jn and TL (SP 'Tixal 1, Gt Harwood 3'). SO,
over railway, then river, and finally canal! Continue to T-jn at memorial
(Tixal) and TL, (no SP). SO, along Tixal Rd. Distant Stafford Castle on
L. SO to lights and TR. SO past Weston school to T-jn. TR along A518
(SP Uttoxeter) – care! This main rd can be avoided by broad grass verge,
for the 300m to exit thankfully by TR into small rd, (opposite FP), over
cattle grid. Semi-metalled track at Stafford Lodge. SO, past Chase View,
hard by fence on L, and Staffordshire County Showground. SO to pink
house, which marks jn of track, FP and BW.

2 – 3

At pink ho, TR, along BW, hard by high wall, enclosing wood. Rough grass, thro' BW gate. SO by wall until 100m from its end, thro' gate and diagonally R to BW gate on R side of field, 200m before Upper Hanyards Fm. TL thro' BW gate, dirt track, hard by L of field, barbed wire fence. SO, thro' four gates and thro' fm and last gate to concrete lane, 50m to T-jn.

3 – 4

TR, down ln for 50m. TL thro' BW gate into field (BW SP). SO across open field, no path. Thro' BW gate at far side, 150m from wood on R. BW cuts diagonally R across planted field, but best push R around perimeter, hard by hedge, exiting at BW gate to good track. SO along track, continuing past Tixall Stables on L, to T-jn with lane at Tixall village, opposite church.

4 – 5

TL, SO to the massive Tixall Fm. Opposite is BW (SP), where TR, thro' white gate. SO 30m, gate, to gravel track to bend, but SO here thro' broken gate (no SP) into fine little grass track. 200m, thro' wide gate, then another, SO same line to exit BW at white house to rd at BW (SP to Tixall).

5 – 6

TR, over canal, under rail, to Gt Haywood at T-jn. TR along High St, past St. John's School to Clifford Arms and TR. Past row of white cottages, under bridge, SP 'BW, no motors'. Over bridge to the magnificent Essex Bridge (see front of OS 127 map!), into Shugborough Park. SO along metalled BW, 200m from mansion, past 'Working Fm', over railway. SO thro' BW gate (as lane bends R), SP 'Staffs Way'. SO, thro' copse, 50m to main rd.

6 – 7

TR (CARE!), for $\frac{1}{2}$ml, rising to Punch Bowl, entry to Cannock Chase. TL at this first track, carpark/picnic site. SO, short uphill BW, then delightfully down between silver birches to T-jn of tracks. TL, SP 'Staffs Way'. Nicely down fine track to Stepping Stones, (on L). SO, SP 'War Cemetery 3m', along stream to wooden SP at clearing and track jn. Take

acute TR (no SP), good broad track, SO, leading steadily up to a high point of Chase, and T-jn of tracks at top. TR, along Heart of England Way, easily for 200m to carpark (Freda's Grave).

7 – 8

SO, across metalled track, SP Stepping Stones. SO, down sunken track – all downhill now! SO, past sunken pond on L at jn, SP Heart of England Way. SO down another fine sunken track to next jn and fork L (Heart of England departs R). Continue down to reach rd at 'The Cutting'.

8 – 1

Ignoring rd, TR, metalled track, BW SP. Past Nursing Home, and directly TL. Track leads gently down to reach rd in 150m. TR, 10m only, and TR back into the start. A short sampler of Park and Chase that offer very fine riding indeed!

Crossing the Essex Bridge, linking Shugborough to the manorial estate, en-route for Cannock Chase (route 22)

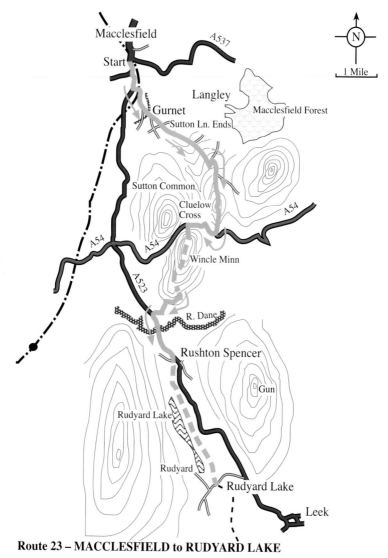

Route 23 – MACCLESFIELD to RUDYARD LAKE

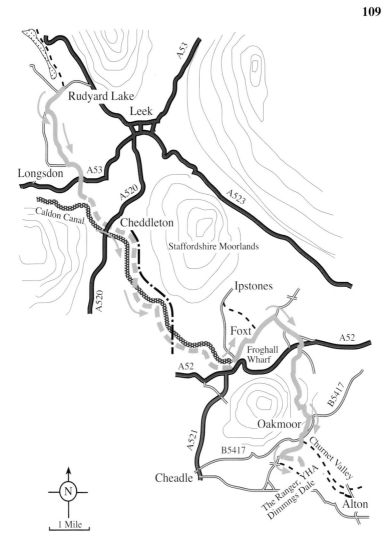

Route 23 – RUDYARD LAKE to ALTON (YHA)

Route 23   (out) **Macclesfield to Alton**

Distance:	33mls.
Off-road:	40%
Height gain:	2475 feet
Time:	5hrs.
Grade:	Difficult (-)
Rating:	***
Refreshments:	Café at start (Tesco), and town, café/pubs around route (see text), including Rudyard, Froghall Wharf, Oakamoor & Alton.
Railway :	Macclesfield (start).
Start:	Station; or Tesco carpark, GR: 920741.
Map:	LR 118 (Stoke on Trent) & LR 119(Buxton); Explorer 259 (Derby), 1:25 000.

Summary:

(Macc to Rudyard Lake):

From Macc station (or Tesco carpark, half-a-mile along the Middlewood Way), the route soon leads steeply up quiet lanes between Shuttlingsloe and Sutton Tower. Down, then up again, over Wincle Minn before rapidly downhill to the flat trail alongside Rudyard Lake and quintessential Staffordshire red-gritstone village.

(Rudyard Lake to Froghall Wharf):

Froghall Wharf to Alton, (The Ranger, YHA) Quiet, hilly lanes descend to the upper Churnet valley, to join the Caldon Canal path, following it south to Froghall Wharf. Another steep rise on lanes past Foxt finally descends back to the Churnet at Oakamoor; then up to The Ranger in glorious Dimmingsdale, and nearby Alton.

Route:

Macclesfield to Rudyard Lake

From Tesco's carpark TR, along to lights in 50m, across to pick up the Middlewood Way track as it follows above the stream. Under the large, low bridge and to the junction – across is the station, Nags Head on R, and town centre up the hill behind.

SO past the station along Sunderland St., SO at the first lights, then TL at next lights, (SP A523, Leek). SO for 150m to next lights and TR (SP Leek, A523). SO, past several rds, to TL at SP (Sutton 1¼, Langley 2, Wincle 5), into Byrons Ln.

SO, past Old King's Head (pub since 1695), James Brindley's House, and under one of his aqueducts (clue to industrial history touched throughout this route). At fork keep L (SP Langley 1), rising gently on Langley Rd to the Church House (tempting pub), where fork R, now steeply up Ridge Hill.

Rapidly gaining height and views, (L – Tegg's Nose, R – Sutton Tower). Past Higher Sutton (fine sign), to the next stiff uphill, following SP 'Cheshire Cycleway' around acute bend. Then SO, shortly past the Hanging Gate, perhaps having earned a pause here. Steadily up to high point, views L – Shutlingsloe (506m) and R – Sutton Tower (402m). SO, short downhill to X-rds. TR (A54, SP Congleton), past Fourways Motel, and Cluelow Cross atop hill on R. Follow A54 down, around bend (SP Congleton, Macclesfield), then uphill, Sutton Tower ahead, to crest.

TL into metalled track, over cattle grid, SP 'Gritstone Trail', FP. Up fine little track, open then walled, past Fm, over high point of Wincle Minn – fine views all around. Descend, following metalled track, thro' three gates, sweeping rapidly down, exiting Minn End Ln at the A523. TL, towards Leek. Down, over the River Dane, escaping by first TR, down little, unmarked lane for 50m to bridge under track. TR, short carry up to the track.

TR, following the broad track, stony at first, towards Rudyard. SO to cross the ln at The Knot Inn, following the trail, (start of route 13, Rushton Spencer). SO, along the fine trail, (light mud in winter) and alongside the lake and miniature railway, continuing past the end of the lake to the rail terminus and carpark that connects to Rudyard village, across the lake. Allow 2 hrs from start.

Rudyard Lake to Froghall Wharf

From the carpark, TL and under the track, then uphill to Rudyard. TL at The New Galleon. Nicely down, SO to TL at the fork, (SP Longsdon 2, Leek 4). Sharp rise, SO, long rd, finally to T-jn. TL (SP Longsdon $^{1}/_{2}$, Leek $2^{1}/_{2}$).

Down to X-rds at Longsdon, The Wheel (pub). SO, superb downhill swoop, over the first waterway, to the second, where TL, down the bank to join the Caldon Canal towpath, (NB, see 'Rights of Way, Canal Towpaths, page 15).

TL, following the canal (southeast) towards Froghall Wharf, Staffs Way, from Bridge 27. Towpath surface past Bridge 31 improves, leading to The Red Lion and Bridge 44 – the Flint Mill museum, this supplied the Potteries with essential ingredients for china ware. SO, soon out to the country, Boat Inn; passing on the left hillside the spectacular motorcycle scramble course, perhaps with free viewing! Railway track reached, as pass SP 'Chase Wood', then The Black Lion. SO, along semi-metalled track to T-jn at SP Compsall Nature, Spring Meadow.

TL, bridge high over canal and railway, as track leads back down to canal. Cross at Bridge 52 and pleasantly alongside canal, eventually crossing rd and SO short track to the carpark, preserved high kilns and refreshment stop at Froghall Wharf – see the info boards for history. (Allow 2 hrs.)

Froghall Wharf to Alton (The Ranger, YHA)

From Froghall Wharf refreshments cottage, TR. Steeply up, heading out of the valley, towards the fine little village of Foxt. L at the fork, and past the appealing Fox & Goose, continuing to gain height, past Foxt church. Down to X-rds where TR (SP Oakamoor 4). Steady rise, to 2nd rd on R, where TR, (small grass triangle). After $^{1}/_{4}$ ml SO over A52. Past stone bus shelter, downhill, SP Cotton $^{1}/_{2}$, Oakamoor 3. SO 150m, then TR, nicely down, SO, tiny twisting lane to T-jn. TL. Down to T-jn, TL (exiting Blakeley Ln). Down 1-in-5 hill to T-jn at Oakamoor.

TR, past The Cricketer's Arms, over the River Churnet, picturesque setting. Note – last stop before the YH, (self catering). TL immediately, at Admiral's House Hotel. Easily down past carpark, (start of

route 18, Churnet Valley). SO to 1ˢᵗ TR and up hill. At top, TL along track to YHA, (SP), reaching it after ¹/₂ml metalled track, with final 150m woodland – delightful rural setting.
(Allow 1 hr)

Track of disused railway line from The Knot Inn, Rushton Spencer to Rutyard, after Rutyard Lake (route 23, out)

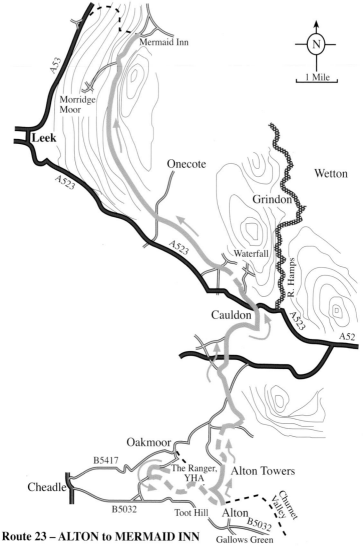

Route 23 – ALTON to MERMAID INN

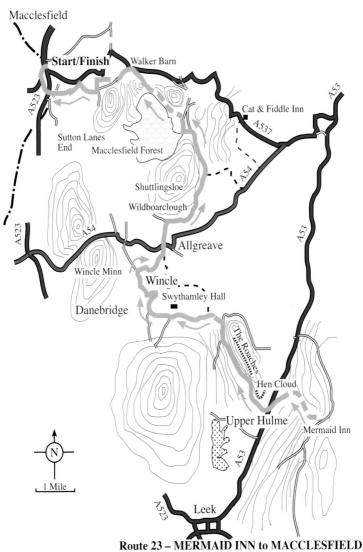

Macclesfield

Start/Finish

Walker Barn

Cat & Fiddle Inn

A537

A523

Sutton Lanes
End

Macclesfield Forest

A54

Shuttlingsloe

Wildboarclough

Allgreave

A54

A523

Wincle Minn

Wincle

A53

Danebridge

Swythamley Hall

The Roaches

Hen Cloud

Upper Hulme

Mermaid Inn

A53

N

1 Mile

Leek

A523

Route 23 – MERMAID INN to MACCLESFIELD

Route 23   (return) **Alton to Macclesfield**

Distance:	39mls.
Off-road:	25%
Height gain:	3225 feet
Time:	7 - 8hrs.
Grade:	Difficult (+)
Rating:	**
Refreshments:	Café/pubs in Alton, and around route (see text), including Yew Tree (Cauldon), Mermaid Inn, Upper Hulme / Roaches, Wincle, Wildboarclough and the excellent Macclesfield.
Railway :	None – until reach Macclesfield.
Start:	The Ranger (YHA); Alton or Oakamoor; GR: 053436 (YHA)
Map:	LR 119(Buxton) & LR 118 (Stoke on Trent); Explorer 259 (Derby) & White Peak, 1:25 000.

Summary:
(Alton to The Mermaid Inn):
    Follow the Churnet Valley route, or directly down through the Dimmings Dale woodland to Alton, crossing the Churnet and rising stiffly past Alton Towers, passing The Yew Tree Inn at Cauldon. A long ride into the heart of the Staffordshire Moorlands eventually reaches the third-highest pub in England, The Mermaid Inn on Morridge Moor.
(Mermaid Inn to Danebridge):
    Descending, the moor leads around The Roaches (nearby farm tea shop), then down again to the valley, marking the Cheshire border, at Danebridge (The Ship Inn beckons).
(Danebridge to Macclesfield):
    The last, long, leg dips in and out of the Dane valley, around the other side of Shutlingsloe and the final track summit at Macclesfield Forest – with fine views to The Cat & Fiddle (second highest pub),

Kerridge Hill, Manchester and Winter Hill far beyond. The descent, via Walker Barn, finds a fine little track before suddenly dropping on back roads into Macc, within a mile from the original start. Satisfied?

Route:

Alton (YHA) to Mermaid Inn (Morridge Moor)

From The Ranger, return to the Oakamoor rd. TL, (following route 18 to the Churnet at Alton), down the rd to Old Furnace. TL, (SP Dimmingsdale, BW). Nicely down, R at fork, following BW SP. Alongside pools, SO at branch, SO at bridge, on between wall and bank, past Dimmingsdale Mill, to T-jn with large track, at Earls Rock. TR, past lake to café 'Rambler's Retreat', (possible breakfast stop). *Alternatively, from The Ranger return 150m and acutely TR down the first track (FP SP – actually BW), following it delightfully down to the track jn. SO down to meet the other way at Earls Rock.*

TR, BW beside the café, SO, gently rising, excellent track. SO, (instead of R as route 18 departs). Continue, down easily to meet rd again. SO, past Toothill Wood to follow Red Rd past coffee shop and Talbot Inn (18th C) to T-jn with bridge crossing the Churnet, (R is Alton). TL, over bridge and up Farley Ln. Past trade, then main, entrance to Alton Towers (hidden by the dense woodland), to T-jn with latter.

SO, into 'No Thro' Rd' (L goes to Farley). Along the metalled lane, and as it bends R, keep L, faded BW SP. Semi-metalled track towards Haybank Fm. At Fm, on L is FP, and continue just to its R, thro' wide metal gate (no SP). SO for 20m to fork, to keep R, down lower track (yellow arrow on black – but **is** BW). Track followed OK, SO gate; not unpleasant and all rideable but under-used, and could be harder work in wet. SO to huge metal gate, exiting to open field, (SP on tree ahead). Traverse field diagonally R and, once over the rise, faith rewarded as metalled track is revealed. Keep L, over cattle grid and past Longshaw Fm, (if gate locked, side gate allows exit alongside), SO to T-jn with rd.

TR, then SO (past two gated and locked tracks on L), for another 50m and TL into wide, stony track, (no SP). Thro' gate and gently rise to exit BW 50m after curious 'sliding pole' gate, BW SP, to T-jn with rd.

TL, then SO (over B5417). At next rd TR, into Cauldon Low (meaning high point hereabouts!). SO (over A52) at The Cross (pub), heading to Cauldon and Waterhouse carpark/picnic site, handy for nearby Manifold Trail – arguably finest valley in Staffordshire, but inside the Peak, of course. Before reaching Cauldon, improbably sited near the limestone works is possibly the most interesting, surely the most unusual pub in this book, if not the land – The Yew Tree Inn – don't miss it!

At T-jn, TL. Follow A523 (care!) to take 1st R, SP 'Waterfall 1', along Waterfall Ln. first TL at school, into Cross Ln. Small metalled ln rises, and becomes unmetalled, but good track, finally reaching a T-jn with the rd. TL, along 50m and TR, SP 'Ford, Onecote'. SO at next four X-rds, digging in for the long haul on this quiet road marking the Peak District boundary, as it rises interminably to Morridge Moor and T-jn at high point of 1519ft. TR, (ignoring minor R) to shortly reach The Mermaid - downhill slightly!

The Mermaid to Danebridge

At The Mermaid TL, (BW gate and SP) to descend the moor in the direction of the distant, but unmistakable profile of Hen Cloud and The Roaches. Follow R of the mangled track, on grass, gently down at first. Down a decent track, then TR thro' the curious BW gates (this reverses section 2 – 3, route 14). Open ground, heading hopefully down the grassy crest to steep ground and grassy track, to ford the stream at woodland edge. Follow BW SPs, thro' small gates and wall, gentle rise. Head for barn, then thro gate 30m to its R. SO, and a decent track thankfully develops, leading thro' Little Swainsmoor Fm. SO, down easily and thro' Swainsmoor Fm, continuing on gravel track, gate, and so finally up steady rise to main rd, (A53 – CARE!).

TL, quickly down 200m, TR and past Ye Olde Rock Inn, at Upper Hulme. At jn, acute TR, and follow the twisting rd as drops down thro' the industrial units then rises on a tough pull up to Hen Cloud, (Roaches Tea Room opposite – perfect position!), followed by an easier gradient past The Roaches. Past the Five Clouds, outcropping further along, and eventually SO past the L turn (from Meerbrook, visited on route 14, section 1 - 2). Up again, not far, then TL into track, SP 'Clough

Head', (re-joining route 14, section 4 – 5). SO, nice grassy way along-side wall, leaving via BW gate, (SP 'Roche End'), to metalled ln.

TL, down pleasant ln to T-jn. TR (leaving route 14), and past Swthamley Park, ³/₄ml to next T-jn. TR, and down to the crossing of the Dane at Danebridge. A popular spot, the rd rises steeply, shortly passing the delectable Ship Inn, en-route for Wincle.

Danebridge to Macclesfield

SO up from Danebridge, to TR at Wincle Church. Down, then steeply up (again!), SO (over A54 – care!). Along the line of the Dane, SO (past rd from the Hanging Gate; see early part of route 23-out), and Nabb Quarry carpark. Down to follow the Dane, past The Crag Inn. SO (past R – Buxton 6, bridge with plaque to Wildboarclough flood of 1989). Past several unobtrusive carparks (access for Shutlingsloe – FP only). SO, winding along the valley until finally reach TL at SP 'Forest Chapel ³/₄', steeply up to corner of Macclesfield Forest.

TR, immediately past 'Standing Stone carpark'. SO, (to R are fine views to distant Cat & Fiddle), to 1ˢᵗ TL, following SP 'Macc. Forest ¹/₄ (chapel)'. Over rise and down to T-jn. Directly ahead is the gritstone walled and surfaced track.

SO, rideable part way up, superb track that bounds the northern aspect of Macc. Forest. Over the high point (1558ft), superb views over Peak and Cheshire, and easily down to track T-jn. TR, and around corner becomes metalled ln. Superbly down to T-jn with A537 Buxton Rd.

TL (CARE!) at Peak millstone boundary marker, to 2ⁿᵈ rd TL, at Walker Barn, following SP 'Tegg's Nose'. Past Walker Barn Methodist Church (never-to-be-forgotten penultimate check, on the annual 56-ml Bullock Smithy Fell Race around the White Peak). Over the rise, and down 75m to TR into the last track, opposite Windyway House. SP 'Gritstone Trail', (which immediately departs across field). SO to end of fine track at T-jn. TL, past Bonny Catty Fm, down to T-jn. TR, short rise and down again towards central Macc, to TL into Blakelow Rd., (just before reaching the A537). Follow this quiet rd across, then down contours, over canal, past The Dolphin, to exit Windmill Ln at T-jn with the London Rd, (remember this?). Opposite is The Sun Inn.

TR, retracing outward journey. Fork L directly. SO to lights. TR, leading back past Macc station, SO under bridge to start of Middlewood Way for Tesco carpark; greeted, in all probability, with a modicum of relief? An outing – especially if done in a single bash – to be savoured in retrospect.

Route 24   (out & return) **Macc. to Alton to Macc.**

Distance:	72mls.
Off-road:	33%
Height gain:	5700 feet
Time:	12 - 13hrs.
Grade:	Severe (-)
Rating:	***
Refreshments:	See routes 23 out and 23 return
Railway :	None – until reach Macclesfield.
Start:	Macclesfield (route 23 out)
Map:	LR 118 (Stoke on Trent) & LR 119(Buxton)

Summary:

See previous two routes. As a grand finalæ, routes 23 – out and return –
fit naturally together, providing a suitable challenge for the sufficiently
experienced with a penchant for endurance tests – an early start and late
finish make this an outing for a fit party around midsummer.

Route:

Follow the previous two routes, as described – good luck!

EPILOGUE

Just before going to press, Pete and I, nobly supported by Martin, rode route 24 on a memorable and almost dry Friday night during an awful spell of July weather. A near-summer solstice ride; we began as darkness fell – 10.30pm from Tescos in Macclesfield. Seeing easily enough by head-torch over the hills past Sutton Tower and Wincle Minn. (albeit with prior-knowledge assisting route finding)

Midnight, the Knot Inn at Rushton Spencer was a welcome light in a dark and surprisingly cold land. Past Rudyard Lake and over the hill to Cheddleton – relieved to have explored the wrong canal (to Leek!) on a sunny day.

Feeble signs of a low moon en-route to a pleasant, if chilly, small hours seat at Froghall Wharf. A stiff climb out of the Churnet increased our temperature then down to Oakamoor and back up to Dimmingsdale YHA as glimpses of dawn's first light entered the sky.

Still darkly down through thick summer vegetation to Earls Rock. Alongside the Churnet to a pause at Alton Bridge opposite the Gothic castle which aptly emerged from the mist, catching early light.

We escaped the Churnet Valley and passed Alton Towers – early visitors on a lonely vigil some four hours before opening! Beyond the rather under-used bridleway, benefiting from the dawn light and on to breakfast, alfresco, courtesy of Martin who plied us with toast, (real) tea and muesli at Waterhouses fine NT carpark.

Convinced that this would be a jolly good finishing point, we nevertheless were committed to continue into the heart of the Staffordshire Moorlands. Slacking perceptibly, we dodged nasty skies over Morridge Moor.

Down to Danebridge and up to Wincle, cheerily greeted by steady flow of cyclists, as mountain and touring bike riders puffed or pushed up into the hills. By the time the Dane is regained and followed past Wildboarclough nothing can stop one finishing – although the track up to Macclesfield Forest makes a good attempt ...

Down to Walker Barn, the last rise soon disposed of and virtually freewheel now, 'comfortably' back around midday (surely a time difficult not to beat). Immediate relief, refreshments, and gathering glow of satisfaction – the café stop at last!

Footnote - supplement to 'Gearing Up' (page 12)

As with any mountain bike expedition, safety and comfort should be of paramount importance. A night ride such as route 24 should only be undertaken by fit and technically capable riders.

If you decide on riding this route we recommend that each member of the group use a head or handlebar mounted lighting system providing at least 12 watts of Halogen equivalent light with battery power to last through the dark hours. Also that you carry a space blanket & lightweight bivvy bag; a first-aid kit; fleece and waterproof clothing; a mobile phone; a flask and plenty of high energy food.

And finally, though possibly most importantly, that you take the time to sit down on a suitable vantage point with your flask and enjoy dawn's first light.

Ours was Alton bridge, providing a fine view of the gothic Alton castle silhouetted against the dawn sky, surrounded by mist – more reminiscent of Transylvania than Staffordshire!).

Why do we need the Air Ambulance?

Though mountain biking isn't a high-risk sport, crashes, and plain old bad luck do affect us all. Mostly the damage is only injured pride, we get back on the bike and ride away. Occasionally it's more serious than that. When it happens we can only dial 999 on a mobile phone and hope. In many cases that hope is for a helicopter. The Air Ambulance Service is our safety net – mountain bikers know that. They have no state funding and depend on donations. We need them and they need us. RUSS is the vehicle through which we thank them and give our support. The Air Ambulance service is our safety net. Mountain bikers know that and RUSS is the vehicle through which we acknowledge it by giving them our support.

The RUSS Appeal

In March 2003 due to no fault or error of his own, Russ Pinder crashed on the Gap descent in the Brecon Beacons – one of his favourite trails. He broke his back and will be in a wheelchair for the rest of his life The Mountain Bike Community responded in a wonderful and humbling way. RUSS Appeal started right there, when Russ asked that any donations made should be directed to Air Ambulance. In the last year it raised an amazing £30,000 and started one of the best MTB events on the calendar.

RIDERS UNITED IN SERIOUS SITUATIONS

RUSS **Trail** *Break*

MOUNTAIN BIKERS PUTTING SOMETHING BACK

Get Involved

+44 (01793) 638639

www.russ-appeal.org.uk

The Ernest Press Mountain Bike Guide series

Inverness, the Great Glen & the Cairngorms: **£8.50**

North Wales: **£8.25**

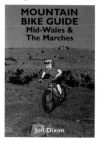

Mid-Wales & the Marshes: **£7.50**

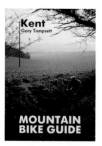

Kent: **£6.95**

Wiltshire: **£8.50**

County Durham: **£7.50**

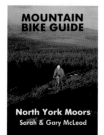

North York Moors: **£7.50**

Northumberland: **£7.50**

Browse and buy online at <u>www.ernest-press.co.uk</u>

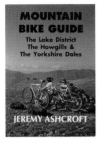

The Lake District, Howgills & Yorkshire Dales: **£7.95**

More routes in the Lakes, Howgills & ... **£7.50**

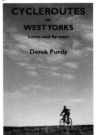

Cycleroutes in West Yorks – Lanes and by-ways: **£7.50**

West Yorkshire: **£7.50**

Mid Yorkshire, Rye Dale & the Wolds: **£7.50**

West Midlands: **£8.00**

East Midlands: **£7.95**

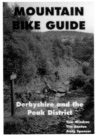

Derbyshire and the Peak District: **£7.50**

The Peak District & Derbyshire: **£7.50**

Breaking *loose*

'The mass of men lead lives of quiet desperation', and few realise their dreams of escape. Dave Cook followed his dream and in 1989 set off for Austrailia on his bicycle. His vivd account tells of his rock-climbing adventures en route, of friends made and of the political situations he found – including a tangle with Saddam Hussein's police. Throughout he records his reflections on social injustice from Yugoslavia to the Indian continent.

Hardback, ISBN 0 948153 26 1, 201 pages - £9.50 - Hardback